Crest To C
The Boo..... ....

MW00963326

William Thorsell

Toronto

To my grandparents, whose spark and grit made so much possible.

Thanks to Sam and Lucy Pivnick, young p
they might read such a story
To Jeffrey Simpson, who pushed to see it ꞁ eꞁ ꞁ aꞁ
audience.
To Clive Veroni, who added momentum,
to Brian Rogers, who helped to see it through, and to the
team at Savvy Books who put it together.

With appreciation,

William Thorsell

i am slower than I walk
softer than I speak
weaker than my open arms extended
and
more profoundly moved by love
than knowledge for
in you
i see my own reflection:
touching then
you are my
confirmation

if I am true
within you
there can be
no final
questioning

May, 1972

TABLE OF CONTENTS

PROLOGUE

Every life rolls the dice, dressed in circumstance. No one asks our permission to be born. Should they ask, some might defer – or seek delay for better prospects. Not on offer. We awake to discover we have limited agency over our fates, are destined to die, and the universe itself will fade to a cold vacuum one day. So informed, we get on with it.

This narrative recounts one such life, including the "kitchen sink" in the manner of Norwegian writers, of whom my maternal grandparents were kin. (The Swedish side leaned to more practical matters.) There is much to learn from kitchen sinks, so I hope you may have the patience to spend some time at this one before heading off to the salon, bedroom and penthouse as well. The first part offers considerable social history; the latter more public affairs. So edit this narrative as you will, ignore what appears marginal, go where you want. Not everything matters, or matters to everyone.

I arrived at the front end of the Baby Boomers in North America – a blessed demographic in human history. Better, I arrived in Canada. The current generation may yet be as fortunate, whatever roils the moment.

PART ONE: FIRST CAREERS

THE KID (STARTS LIKE LINCOLN)

I was conceived at a Royal Canadian Air Force base in Claresholm, Alberta, in the fall of 1944, as the Second World War reached its climax (among others). Hitler was alive, and the atomic bomb had not yet been tested. There was much of interest in play just then – time to visit the planet.

Nine months later, on July 6, 1945, I emerged from my mother Irene at St. Mary's Catholic hospital in Camrose, Alberta, 20 miles from New Norway, my parents 'home. Irene had returned to bear her second son (Jim was already four years old). My grandfather drove her to Camrose in a barebones Ford. We were not Catholic, but my first sight was of nuns. That's why I'm gay.

Sivert Westvick, Irene's father, peered into the crib and said, "He looks like a picked crow." My mother burst into tears. That's why I'm single.

By the fall, my dad Arnold and mother were staying with decommissioned air force friends in Wetaskiwin, 20 miles west of Camrose. Arne helped build a garage behind their small house. That's where we spent my first winter alive, huddled around a wood stove except for my parents 'use of the bathroom in the house. Arne told me later that I owed him for the nights he got up to stoke that stove. I was already running a tab. Like Abraham Lincoln, I started life in something of a cabin. Actually, I prefer to think, like Steve Jobs, I got my start in a garage.

The following August, Irene gave birth to my sister Corinne. Irene told me much later that she cried when she found she was pregnant just four months after my birth. Not to say that, like her four sisters, she dreaded telling her Norwegian immigrant mother she was pregnant at any time: Anna Sather Westvick knew where that came from, and was capable of very deep frowns. At the same time, Irene was enormously happy to have a daughter in the family.

By that summer of 1946, we were in Alberta's capital, Edmonton, 40 miles north of Wetaskiwin, renting a small house on 73rd Avenue right across the street from my cousins, the Fieldings. It is here where my own memory starts to kick in describing a typically unlikely life.

***

I had memories at three years old, but have forgotten them. I remembered words and numbers and the faces of my friends and family. All gone. The first memory that made it to later was of fire.

I woke up in my basement room one night, blue flames of the natural gas space-heater flickering against a ceramic back-plate to fight the chill. I watched those flames and realized the ceramic captured and held the heat, just for me. Remarkable.

I recall breaking my nose by jumping off a dresser, curling up in the back of the car on our way to the

3

hospital. I saw blood on the upholstered seat and feared the displeasure of my mother.

An upright piano arrived one afternoon in the small front hall of that house: I spent an eternity that day trying to understand the difference between black and white notes. Focusing on white, I discovered the harmony in thirds.

I got a wooden toy consisting of eight posts of different colours sticking up on one side. You hit them flat to the base with a wooden mallet, turned the toy over and there they were sticking up, waiting to be hit again. I set out to discover how many different patterns of hitting them down existed before the options ran out. As with the piano keyboard, I used this toy to envision numbers and math for years to come.

My dad was building a new house for us in the "Martin Estate" – land on the south edge of Edmonton reserved for veterans eligible for cheap mortgages. We drove across a field, and I saw just one house standing a few places away from the concrete foundation of our own. My dad gave me a paper bag of small nails and a hammer, and asked me to pound nails into the plywood floor already in place on the main level. He disappeared down a ladder to work below, and I set out to "help build" the house, nail by nail. Sometime later, my pounding went silent. Arne snuck up the ladder and saw me sucking my injured thumb, intent on not crying – I do recall not crying. He silently retreated, and my nail-pounding started up soon again. Years later, as he cut my hair in the basement furnace room, I would look up and see all these little nail points sticking down randomly through the wood above. I never hit a beam.

We moved into 5515–109th Street in September, 1949. After sharing my sister's bedroom upstairs, I got my own room in the basement in time for Christmas, near my brother. My space was lined with square wood panels and adjoined the rumpus room, which was dressed with pine boards – and housed the piano. My brother and I shared a bathroom. Just starting my fifth year on the planet, I had my own suite and music studio, brand new and waiting to be explored.

***

How do we fall into patterns of being? What is the relationship between inclination and opportunity that builds an identity, sets boundaries, forms tastes and shapes worldviews? Just past four years old, I had recourse to a lovely little world of my own, starting in that basement, next to the piano, where I could shut the sliding door and fiddle around.

My brother was almost five years older, and our paths crossed really only at meals. My sister lived upstairs in her own pleasant world (though we loved playing board games after dinner). My parents were of Scandinavian heritage, prone to independent living on everybody's part. My mother had been a teacher in a one-room school (Red Willow, outside New Norway).

We were a family, to be sure, though with proper distances understood. My mother stayed home in those early years; there was never a hint of insecurity or risk: Irene was always there. We were each secure on our own together.

We were "middle class" in those days, my father working at a lumberyard predating things such as Home Depot. He came home for lunch. In the hall, there was a little hollow carved out in the wall, with a wire hanging. A year later that would be a telephone: 38390.

***

Television did not arrive for another five years, but we had Amos 'n Andy on the radio, along with The Happy Gang, and a record player. And, of course, the piano.

I was at the keyboard every day, figuring out God Save the Queen and more about the math in music. When I got to Grade One in public school, my mother sent me

6

to a music teacher to start real lessons. I went to the teacher's house, and she proceeded to grab my hands and insist on different fingering etc. I gazed out her living room window as she did this, with growing contempt. Arriving home, I told my mother that if she ever sent me back there, I would never touch the piano again. "No problem," she said, "you're free." I raced to the basement and played the piano for hours.

I have many friends who took all 12 grades in the Royal Conservatory of Music and did very well in their exams. None of them plays the piano anymore. I play and learn and compose on the piano almost every day, now for two or three hours in the morning. My RCM pals say they don't play now because they make too many mistakes, or their technique has fallen down. The perfect has become the enemy of the good, and they have lost the joy in making music (if they had it before the discipline).

How many parallels exist in other fields, especially in our very competitive times? The shambling of the dilettante is no longer much respected, and maybe no longer much enjoyed. People retreat to consumption out of fear of showing amateurism in action, though social media are changing that. "Renaissance Man" has become a term of some disapprobation.

My summer holidays were entirely unstructured. I never wanted to go or went to camp. The neighbourhood filled up with baby boomers, and we all had bicycles. Living at the edge of town, we boys biked for hours into the countryside, to forests, sloughs and birds 'nests. We built warring tree houses and caves alongside Whitemud Creek.

Or we explored the city, crossing the High Level Bridge into downtown and the grounds of the Alberta Legislature. The only rule we faced was "be home for supper."

Once each summer, we organized a "Penny Carnival" in my parents' backyard. We set up camping tents to offer a "House of Horrors" (including canned spaghetti as brains), fortune-telling and games of chance. In the garage, we strung sheets across the parking space, with a bright light behind. Kids would sit on chairs facing this screen as I called for "Leonardo, Leonardo!" to rise from the dead (my friend Ellis). His exaggerated shadow would suddenly appear along with low drumming, and he would respond to questions with apocalyptic prognostications. The audience left shaken to the core.

We counted our pennies at the end of the day and bolted down to the UN Market at the corner to buy candy with now-socially toxic names. The summer went on and on.

It is a cliché now to fret about the heavy schedule imposed on kids during summer holidays – camps of every kind: school in another guise. I think "make-your-own-fun" summers gave us great value, not only through the things we explored and created but by the fact we were so autonomous at a young age for two months of the year. I think the latter is often overlooked: A sense of autonomy is hard to acquire after years of relentlessly following directions and meeting expectations. Our sense of autonomy was bred in the bone, summer day after summer day, year after year. You could even decide to reject piano lessons and not go to camp, and follow your muse.

***

School was easy and interesting for me, though I was always uncomfortable with kids who broke the rules. I respected rules. In Grade Three or so, I fearfully saw my mother coming up the sidewalk at school in mid-morning and discovered much later that she was meeting my teachers about me skipping a grade. They decided against it on social grounds: I avoided conflict and would not do well against older bullies. The way things evolved, I was enormously fortunate to stay within my cohort.

**

In 1954, television came to Edmonton. We got the first set in the neighbourhood, a big RCA box perched on four spindly legs, with an antenna on top. The test pattern came on air ten days before the launch of CFRN, and, at nine years old, it was my responsibility to figure out the dials for contrast, horizontal and vertical, as well as the best angle for the antennae. I spent days on the floor playing with the test pattern – an Indian chief in the middle – to ensure good reception on Friday night at 6 pm for CFRN.

The neighbours crammed into our house while I maintained my position on the floor in front of the set. At 6 pm, there was a countdown, and then we saw a black and white moving picture of a man announcing a new era in Edmonton: CFRN! "I Love Lucy," "Ed Sullivan", and "The Millionaire" would ultimately join the news in commanding our attention each evening. One of the first big stories on CBC was Hurricane Hazel in Toronto. A wider world suddenly attended our lives.

In media, we had grown up on books, comics, records, radio, cinema and musical instruments, whose status was not hugely displaced by TV, however. There was only one channel, after all. Scarcity sustained a certain diversity of media then, and so perhaps, modes of perceiving things.

***

We started noticing Judy's breasts in Grade Six. In Grade Seven, we boys started getting itchy penises at night, and our voices broke (the source of much teasing by my aunts). There were separate classes for girls and boys for HPD - Health and Personal Development. When our teacher got to the sex stuff – particularly the internal structure of girls – the room went mad with laughter, derision and curiosity (or, in my case, fear). Our teacher was pretty well shouted down. He limped to retirement before the end of the year.

Being gay then didn't have any meaning and generated little consciousness. There was never a reference in public or private to homosexuality, except in the occasional shout-out of "homo" at some unfortunate guy playing sports, but that was rare. You went through puberty and discovered masturbation. Nothing was said. If you fantasized about boys, you didn't compute it.

Yes, you fooled around with one or two guys from time to time, but there was no weight to the baggage. And then you "grew out of it."

11

Today, a kid like me at that age is fully aware of the gay thing, told to be fine with it and sees many functional role models. And has porno on his computer. It is beyond my imagination to comprehend how that must play out by the high school. My case would turn into a personal civil war.

JUL • 62

Autumn was working season at our house. We had a half-acre with an enormous vegetable garden across the back. We started by digging potatoes, hosing them down in large piles on the lawn, leaving them to dry. Then it was rutabaga and carrots. Beans, spinach and peas were consumed throughout the summer. We had a "cold room" in the basement, which had a hole opening directly to the freezing air outside, with wooden bins on either side. We filled these bins with the root vegetables in layers separated by wood shavings. They lasted until March. My mother canned fruit displayed in glass jars that lined a basement wall.

My father, brother and uncles made three major hunting trips in the fall. The first was for ducks and geese, which they hung by necks on our exterior garage walls – maybe 60 birds in all. We sat and plucked these birds over pails of water after dinner, night after chilly night, before they went to a large freezer in the basement.

The second trip was for pheasant, prairie chicken and grouse in southern Alberta, with the same consequence for cleaning and plucking. The third was for deer, elk and moose. I returned from school to find half-sides of these animals hanging in the garage, still covered with fur. My father spent many nights cutting them up with his saws, wrapping and labelling them in shiny brown paper, and Corinne and I would take those packages down to the freezer. I can still hear my mother saying, "Billy, go to the basement and get two pheasants, four potatoes and three carrots." In the winter, we lived off the land (and skated every day at the community ice rink down the block).

***

HIGH SCHOOL WAVES

As Tevya, 1962

I liked acting, as opposed to acting out. I played Ko Ko in The Mikado in Grade 8, and Gaspar, a grasping villain in Grade 9. I was lighting assistant for The Glass Menagerie in Grade 10, played Falkland in The Rivals in Grade 11, and then hit a wonderful spot as Tevya in Scholom Aleichem's "Tevya and His Daughters" (the book for the musical "Fiddler on the Roof").

I don't know how our drama teacher at Strathcona Composite High, Donald Pimm, chose a Jewish folk-play, and then put me in the lead as Tevya. We presented it up on stage, with intimate stadium seating on either side. I was on-set throughout, an old milkman tending his cow, his family and his god. "Lazar Wolf – you're here, you're not here – it's me, Tevya!" opened the second act, which led to the marriage of Tevya's daughter.

It went so well that we added a third weekend on demand just for the Jewish community in Edmonton, many of whom asked me about my bar mitzvah. I carried many of Tevya's mannerisms and accents with me during the rest of high school to the mirth of my classmates. (The girl who played my wife Golda ended up as Dean of Law at Osgood Hall in Toronto years later – Marilyn Pilkington.)

John W. Bilsland, a drama critic for the Edmonton arts magazine Town Talk, wrote this in his review, May 1962: "This was by far and away the finest of Strathcona Composite's productions this winter, and it was made such by the remarkable performance of Bill Thorsell as Tevya. I had seen this boy once before this winter in The Rivals, and I had not been particularly impressed. As Tevya, however, he revealed great gifts. The part is extremely demanding – Tevya really is the play, and he is on the stage all the time – but Thorsell never once faltered in either of the performances I saw. (I went back for a second try with this one, and it was well worth it.)"

Two years later, in June 1964, I wrote a column about acting in The Vista, the student newspaper of Victoria Vocational High School in Edmonton, from which: "Why would you take drama and risk being classed as an 'oddball 'or a 'queer'? Why did I? Because to me, drama is a golden opportunity to become someone else. I am free from being what and who I am. I have a rare chance to look at the world through someone else's glasses: I am not stifled and inhibited by my own fears and apprehensions, and I can be and do and feel things that are out of reach to just about everybody else.... Through drama, I can get rid of the musty drab coat that I wear from day to day and become an exciting, alive human being.... Drama gives you the opportunity to put on any mask to see how it fits. You have a chance to take the best from each mask and add it to your own unique special mask and make that mask more valuable by far. Go ahead! Take any mask that comes along and check it to see if perhaps it has something that you can use. You can do this through drama. Drama is freedom. Drama is opportunity... Go on! Try the Masks on for size."

What is this? A 19-year-old gay kid seeking some kind of freedom? An honest embrace of what we now call "multiculturalism"? I know just what it is: joy in the fact of irrepressible humanity. (Edward Snowden, in his memoir, speaks of the pleasure he felt in the 1990s, presenting himself anonymously as various identities on the internet, the freedom it gave him to inhabit different versions of himself. And that, I think, helped him to know his true self more deeply – with significant consequences.) Aristotle: "Know thyself."

My mother Irene kept a scrapbook, which I found in her things many years later. It was filled with inspirational clippings from newspapers, some of her own writings, and typed pieces on life lessons. Near the end (1960), was a typed page in upper-case:

"Why am I? Was I put on this earth for some purpose? Or am I just a beast of burden to work and sweat in the fields? The creation of my soul must have some purpose, hidden deep in the subconscious of my mind, and when my opportunity makes it undescernable [sic] appearance, I alone shall see it and grab it, for if I hesitate for, but one second, the chance shall be gone and I will revert to my former status of being but a shadow, a bird among the flock, a fish between the seas.

Bill Thorsell"

Jumping in Grade ten from our neighbourhood Allendale Junior High to Strathcona Composite High School, with 1,700 students, greatly expanded my world. Scona's students were drawn from a wide swath of south-central Edmonton, which included the neighbourhoods around the University of Alberta. Suddenly my peers were sons and daughters of surgeons, bankers, architects and professors who didn't live in the barrio where I grew up. When I visited their houses, I saw worlds with elegant surroundings, libraries and even tea with their fathers beside the fireplace. My own home was among the most comfortable in our area, and my parents were smart and educated. But there was a gentility to these new places that struck me immediately and, of course, demanded emulation. This process of "growing out" would continue apace.

Scona's classrooms were "streamed" by academic and program goals. I was in the "e-stream" (meaning "excellence") with about 20 other students. With the exception of one elective, we "smart kids" stayed together all day for our courses, which were distinct from other matriculation classes also heading to university. (Scona offered automotive, woodworking and "business"

19

streams as well.) By Grade 12, our e-group was something of a family compact, elite if not elitists. (I don't remember looking down on other kids, but who knows.) We took two tailored math courses and a special program in physics from the US, as well as chemistry, social studies, French and English. The one elective we took with everyone else seemed like chaos due to the noise and indiscipline in the room. We preferred our "stream."

In Grade 12, everything focused on the Departmental exams in June, graded anonymously by strangers and counting for 100 percent of the year's marks. By May, we were studying hours each night with much at stake. Then that month, my family moved house.

***

Arne with the Umbaugh U18

My father, Arne, was inventive and imaginative. Beyond work at the lumberyard, he built houses and walk-up apartments on his own time, and even bought a hardware store for a while, where I enjoyed working on Saturdays. He was a pilot and mechanic in the Second World War, played saxophone in the RCAF Big Band, and took up flying again in a two-seat Cessna. Then came the Umbaugh.

(Arne said he was "saved" by the war, where the RCAF wrenched him from rural poverty in the Depression and taught discipline and many skills. He described 1939-45 as the happiest time in his life on that base in Claresholm, Alberta, filled with learning, purpose, love and life-long friendships.)

The Umbaugh – or U18 – was going to be everyman's flying machine. It was a two-seat gyrocopter, with a Lycoming engine on the back and helicopter rotors on top. The rotors served as "wings" for lift, as the Lycoming created speed. If the Lycoming conked out, the U18 would purportedly drift down to earth under its rotors like a maple-tree seed, safely landing wherever.

Arne went to Maryland and bought the rights to sell the Umbaugh in Western Canada and the North. While the company sought FAA approval, he quit his job, rented an office at the Edmonton airport and printed letterhead

(Gyro Aviation). FAA approval arrived, Arne made a bid and went to Maryland with his brother to fly the fourth production model of the U18 home to Alberta.

They ran out of gas somewhere over Michigan. The Umbaugh floated down to a farmer's field, as promised. They bought gas from the flummoxed man, and continued on.

The U18 buzzed loudly over our house on to touchdown at the airport and earned a photo in the Edmonton Journal. I liked hanging around the hangers, with all the planes and hot mechanics. We were going to be rich.

-When Umbaugh went bankrupt a year later, so did Arne, who had apparently taken out a new mortgage on our house. One month before the Grade 12 Departmental exams in June 1963, my mother told me she had bought a house up near the university, and we would be moving in a week. That was all she said – I didn't understand the backstory for some years (as far as I understand it even now). I just needed to get into my new room to study.

***

How could my mother buy a house on her own in 1963?

Irene told me that she had always wanted to be a "downtown Sarah" rather than a housewife living at the edge of town in the suburbs. In the 1930s, she attended Normal School in Camrose to become a schoolteacher. She won an athletic scholarship for summer school at the University of Alberta in 1935, where she lived at Pembina Hall. She and her friends loved walking over the High Level Bridge to downtown, where the action was. Once, returning to campus over the bridge, a man opened his coat to expose himself to the young women. My mother said they were terribly shocked and not entirely appalled.

She was hired as the teacher at a one-room school, grades 1 to 6, in Red Willow, a country corner a few miles outside her home of New Norway. She boarded with a farmer's family across the way. My father courted by driving her back from Sunday dinners at her home in New Norway to Red Willow with a horse and buggy or sleigh. They married in 1938, and thus by regulation, my mother had to quit her job to make way for another single person needing work in the Depression.

Working as a teacher in Red Willow, Irene wrote in longhand a booklet called Picture Study on how to teach art in early grades, from which: "The first aim of art work in the public school should be the development of a

23

consciousness of beauty and its relationship to life – an appreciation of beauty found everywhere... Beauty is one of the great assets of the human race. To provide for practical knowledge and an appreciation of this asset surely is a matter of great importance in education."

When my sister Corinne and I arrived in Junior High (1958), Irene decided to work part-time. She applied for a sales job at Woodward's department store downtown. She went for the interview but threw up in the washroom from nerves and came straight home – an accomplished woman out of practice. Some months later, she applied for a similar position at Eaton's and got through the interview. Thus started her career as a sales person in children's wear.

At some point, she moved to Sears, north of downtown, and would walk all the way there from our house over the High Level Bridge to its location near the airport – at least an hour. She preferred to walk. Then she gathered her courage, with the support of a friend who worked at the Edmonton Public School Board, and became a substitute teacher for grades 1 to 3 all over town. She won so much respect that teachers on medical leave would lobby to have Irene take their class for that extended period. It often happened that she taught full-time in these circumstances.

Irene also played the piano at a dance school downtown on the weekends, where girls were learning to pirouette. One of them wrote me recently out of the blue with memories of Irene's dependable kindness.

All this time, she was saving money on her own account, abetted by her share (among four sisters) of her parents 'estate. She invested in GICs at the Alberta Treasury Branch. None of us had any sense of the scope of her savings. But in the spring of 1963, when my father went bankrupt, and we lost the house that he (and I) had built, Irene had the money to buy another one, just beside the High Level Bridge and a 20-minute walk to the campus of the University of Alberta. If not for my mother then, what would have happened?

I don't think their relationship survived this transition for long. My father went back to construction, bidding on weather stations in the Yukon and Northwest Territories, and would be away for months at a time. Then he became a real estate agent. And then, some years later, he left our house and started another life.

Irene kept working and saving. She gave me $500 to buy a 1957 yellow Pontiac sedan, which virtually became the collective property of my friends. We'd go camping in the Rockies. She kept walking to work.

***

High School Grad

In the spring of 1962, finishing Grade 11, I ran for President of the Student's Council at Scona. My friends and I mounted a fierce campaign, making enormous posters out of brown paper rolls in my parents' basement. One of them hung vertically down two stories from a window near the entrance of the school. I won.

Grade 12 was wonderful. My friends held the best posts in student government, and even excelled at sports. Our social lives were jammed with parties in basements and new music coming out of the UK. My friend Dave Macfarlane had a sports car and picked me up each morning to drive to school. My new buddies, Bob Reece and Cam Little, lived near the university and, now that I had a driver's license, I could fetch them in my dad's car at 9:30 pm after homework for a burger at the A&W. Better, Dave Macfarlane would come by with his dad's pink Cadillac with those famously high fins, and we'd dominate the A&W parking lot, all windows down, radio turned up loud.

At graduation, Cam was President of the Graduating Class, I was President of the Student's Union, and the world was right. I won the prize for "outstanding" student, which came with a collection of Shakespeare's plays that I still treasure. Then came those exams.

We sat for seven three-hour exams the last week of June. After the last one, Cam and I climbed to the top of the bell tower at the Alberta Legislature and carved our initials into the sandstone. (Are they still there?) Three weeks later, the fateful letter came to us all with our final marks.

That Saturday morning, we were meeting at a local church for some kind of day trip. Everybody asked about their marks. I replied 89.3. No, they said, the average of your marks! I replied 89.3. All my marks in the maths and sciences were in the 90s; French and social studies pulled me down in the 80s.

A week later, I received a letter from the University of Alberta saying that, as one of two top students in the province, I had won a scholarship that would pay my undergraduate tuition as long as my grades held up. I never paid a penny in tuition through the following seven years in universities. Given all those scores in the 90s, I enrolled in Honours Chemistry. Classes started in September 1963, after a different kind of summer.

***

UNIVERSITY OF ALBERTA BLOOMING

I took my first full-time summer job just turning 18 (on July 6) at Vetch Bros. Construction as a labourer. (The Vetches were friends of my parents and lived in our old neighbourhood.) I reported to the site of a new food market (still there on 99th street) under a bright sun. The foundation was in place and they gave me a pole comprised of two-by-fours and handles to pound down the infill around the exterior of the foundation. By noon, without a hat and having been confined to my dark room for months, I had something like sunstroke.

I crawled into the tub back home at the end of the day, red and aching. I wore a hat the next day.

It turned out to be an interesting job, which saw me driving a pick-up truck to the dump filled with construction debris, shovelling gravel into basements, scraping concrete floors in a new nunnery, and piling lumber just so beside the church. (The nuns gave me their homemade cookies.) I was astounded to get my first cheque for $200 later in July – a moment of passage in a young man's life. By the end of August, I was in good physical and mental shape, and the guys at Vetch gave me a party by the cement-mixer on my last day at work. I had my first beer and knew how to drive a loaded pick-up.

***

My best friends Cam and Bob decided to take a year off working in Germany before attending U of A, so I arrived pretty much on my own. I was reading Catcher in the Rye on a bench in the quad when a guy approached, saying he had known my brother, who was now at business school at Western. His name was Paul Cantor and he was president of the Delta Upsilon fraternity. Would I be interested in "rushing" to become a member?

I gave an immediate no, realizing I would be very uncomfortable in a jock-like frat house. "But it's the mansion over there on Saskatchewan Drive, built by Ernest Rutherford, the first Premier of Alberta!" he said. Then he told me that DU was not a secret fraternity and didn't discriminate against Jews. I hadn't heard of such discrimination and was rather perplexed. Rutherford House was just across the way. Paul convinced me to walk over right then just to look inside.

Beyond white columns on the front porch, an oak double-staircase curved up from the panelled entry, and a library gleamed to the left, still holding many of Rutherford's books in cases around the fireplace. An ample salon graced the other side, and a large dining room sat 30, with lunch and dinner made by an onsite cook.

Bedrooms filled the top two stories, and a big party room filled the basement. Antiques graced the corners and prints adorned the walls. I agreed to rush DU on the spot. It became my social base for the next three years.

(I met "big brother" Paul Cantor in later life when he appeared at an editorial board meeting of The Globe and Mail as head of CIBC's investment bank. Our paths crossed regularly then in Toronto until his passing in 2018.)

***

It is amazing I had no awareness of discrimination against Jews in 1963 and indeed did not know who was Jewish among my friends. Obviously, we hadn't learned about that in school, and ethnic/cultural differences just didn't make much of a mark in our neighbourhood growing up. Some friends went to Catholic school, but we had no view on that: It was just the way things were (though the Catholics were banned from doing the twist at their school dances). For a time in the 1950s, we became aware of "DPs" – Displaced Persons arriving as refugees from Europe – and would sometimes mock their lack of English or the smell of garlic on their breath. But that soon became unfashionable and passed.

The only time I saw a black person until university (and rarely then) was when a black family walked past our house one Sunday afternoon, heading for downtown. We were dumbfounded, and never saw them again. We saw indigenous people only on trips to Pigeon Lake or Calgary when we passed through a Reserve. We'd press our faces against the car window, struck by their poverty and isolation from our world. There was no sense of shared space, history or future.

At the U of A, there was similar indifference to ethnic and cultural variety, perhaps because there was so little expression of it in people's appearance, class and behaviours. You might ascribe it to the homogeneity of society through the 1950s – just about everybody was of European stock finding their feet again after the war - or you might call it an innocent form of liberalism at a time when identity issues simply languished in the Alberta I knew. Pre-Post-Modernist, we were just friends from indistinct backgrounds in my experience. That started to change later in the decade with the Counterculture, but I lived ignorant of these kinds of distinctions – some might say ignorantly – and that is who I was at that age. We took every individual at face value and went from there, which is, in fact, not so ignorant at all.

At the same time, I was already steeling myself against too much social intercourse. Starting university in 1963, I wrote "The Case Against Love," from which: "Dependence breeds weakness, and since love breeds dependence, it breeds weakness. A man in love is essentially weaker than a man who is not because the man in love is more dependent... If a man wishes to be truly great, he must thrust aside the temptation of falling in love, to ensure that his love will not interfere with the attaining of his goals."

In the id, I was preparing for the solitude of being gay, perhaps.

***

Another guy rushing DU turned out to be Tom Radford, and we bonded immediately over our love of the humanities. I was in chemistry and he was in history, but we shared a passion for philosophy, history and politics. Tom was the grandson of Bulmar Watt, once editor of the Edmonton Journal, and came from a deeply English family that lived on the north side. His mother was distilled in classic English virtues and tastes, including oriental rugs and Chinoiserie. His father represented Seagram's and English gin, of which there was always an ample supply on my visits there for dinner. It was another exotic world, unusually cultured and rich in colour and history. I imbibed.

Tom and I shared a passion as well for Alberta and even the winter weather. We'd stand on Saskatchewan Drive looking north to the arrival of the first blizzard at minus 20 Fahrenheit in November – and cheer it on. This was our space and time, this winter onslaught, bred in the bone and the bone much better for it. More about Radford later, who remains an historic friend, though our views of winter have diverged somewhat.

**

We were required to take phys-ed in the first year, which I disliked (except for the guy in my class who was cruelly handsome in the change room). I was swimming lengths in the pool at noon one November Friday when someone signalled: "President Kennedy has been shot in Dallas."

A few minutes later, I walked into the crammed cafeteria of the Student's Union Building where loudspeakers were tuned to the radio and heard that he was dead. I went on to my botany class, where we dissected mice. Then I walked home to watch television.

For us, Dallas was the real opening shot of the 1960s. It ripped a tear in our assumptions and drove a stake into our emotions. The murder of Lee Harvey Oswald, the next morning, caught live on TV in Texas, compounded the sense of disbelief. Then there were days of coverage of Kennedy's funeral, in black and white, and hours of grief on the couch watching it all pass by under barren trees. For me and many of my friends, this was our first great loss, our first exposure to real danger (except the prospect of nuclear bombs), our first notice to be on guard in a world whose security and pleasures we had always assumed.

The following year was not too bad: President Johnson's Civil Rights and Great Society programs swept through, and he was easily elected that fall. The Beatles appeared on Ed Sullivan as the "English wave" broke over North American culture. Parties in the DU basement were electrified by live bands, new beats and spiked drinks. And I decided to change course quite dramatically.

***

It was Philosophy 240 that did it. The Science faculty required us to take one elective in the humanities. I took Philosophy 240 – a survey course starting with Athens.

To access the books, I had to use the Reading Room in Rutherford Library instead of the science floor in the new Cameron Library.

At Rutherford, I found myself immersed in Socrates, Plato, Descartes and Hume, gazing up through enormous windows under elegant chandeliers, losing myself in ancient arguments. I started saving up time from my science studies to spend more on Phil 240. I imbibed Plato's lessons, the most powerful being the "proof" that when you set out to harm someone else, you always harm yourself more. I was hooked.

In a fateful move, I informed my chemistry professor I was going to switch from Science to Arts and take a degree in History (the three-year degree, not the four-year honours). He was unhappy, which led to a meeting with the Dean of Science in his beautifully panelled office. It would be a great waste, they said, for me to leave science for history. I could have history on the side, with science still at the centre. I had a promising future in science.

I thought it over for a week or two and chose history right after Christmas.

It was decisive, not only because it altered the course of my studies, but the combination of history and choice of the three-year degree meant I would graduate in 1966 rather than 1967. Who knew how important that would turn out to be for my career and life?

***

I was ready to return to Vetch Bros. as a labourer in the summer of 1964, looking forward to more macho development and that pick-up truck. I don't recall how this happened, but I also noticed the Edmonton Tourist Bureau building on the south entrance to town on Highway 2, coming up from Calgary (probably because it was just across the highway from the A&W). I went down to City Hall and applied for a summer position at the Tourist Bureau, where I assumed they might need more staff. A bewildered guy interviewed me, saying they didn't hire summer students.

A few days before June 1, when I would start at Vetch, they called to say I was hired at the Tourist Bureau. I would be an information officer on the desk directing tourists on how to get to Jasper Avenue, or Jasper Park, or on up to the Alaska Highway.

I loved the assignment and the two women who worked there permanently liked my company. When I returned to U of A that fall, they hired me to cover Sundays alone at the Tourist Bureau through the winter.

So I had a new part-time job, in addition to free tuition and living free in my parents 'house. I was saving money.

One winter Sunday afternoon, setting out to walk home from the tourist bureau– a dark hour in the cold – I heard on the radio of Winston Churchill's death. I lost myself in thought about him on that walk and concluded we were both somewhat bull-headed.

***

Bob Reece and Cam Little returned from Europe and rushed DU to join Radford and me that fall, one year behind us in school. We became four fast friends, double-dating and hanging out. Somehow, we got interested in making movies and acquired 8mm cameras that would accommodate a five-minute reel. We set up competing "film companies," mine with Cam called "Litthor Productions," and theirs called "RWMR/TBER Productions" (based on initials). We created signs and pasted them on the sides of our respective cars.

Every month or two, we hosted an awards ceremony to premiere our latest five-minute film. The trophy was an illuminated Statue of Liberty, revolving at the centre of a 33 RPM record player. Our friends would come to someone's basement, drink beer and await the screenings, prepared to vote.

Litthor's first production was called "The Carnivore" and opened with a shot of the moon hovering over Cam wielding a butcher knife as he crept into a house to murder and ate the occupant. Canned spaghetti again appeared in theatrical use. The Carnivore was accompanied on the stereo by Mussorgsky's "Night on Bald Mountain."

Tom and Bob's premiere, "Love," opened with an impressionistic shot through a fish tank with Tchaikovsky in the background, and starred Tom and his girlfriend Muffy drifting in slow motion on the way to a kiss at the five-minute mark. (This scene became known infamously as the "meeting of the mucus," given the extreme close-up of its climax.)

I forget who won that first competition, but I do recall that "The Carnivore" was a hit at the DU fraternity some months later. We hosted seven or eight such premieres, and the films (which could not be edited except in real-time while shooting) grew in complexity and imagination. ("See How They Run" starred Anne Wheeler, of whom more later.) Who knew these enthusiasms would grow into an influential Western Canadian film group a few years hence?

***

Tom, Cam, Bob and I were returning from a movie downtown across the High Level Bridge when the talk turned to girlfriends. Bob was dating someone seriously, and Tom and Cam were on their way. Bob was questioning how significant this really was: Maybe he'd invoke the "let's go camping" test to see how much resilience existed in their relationship. Sitting in the back seat watching the black bridge girders go by, this conversation struck me straight-on: I was going to lose them: I was going to lose my buddies to girls, and nothing could be done. I felt the shadow of loneliness I had not felt before.

Radford and I as Yearbook Editors, 1965

In 1965-66, Radford and I were in a sweet spot of sorts. Somehow, we were co-editors of The Green and Gold, the University of Alberta's annual yearbook. We decided to build on it. The yearbook was usually just headshots. We kept that, and decided to add "campus life" in our 1965-66 edition. We decided to be journalists.

That meant using photographers to document "real life" in all the faculties, fraternity houses and streets throughout the year: Parties. Labs. Arguments. Graduations. Parties again.

And it meant capturing the spirit of the campus as a whole, starting with autumn in the quad and then winter-white outside the Rutherford Library. This yearbook would record more than faces – it would capture spirits and intuitions. Our radical yearbook won the national prize that year.

As it happened, I also became the co-chair (with Myrna Kostash) of Varsity Guest Weekend (VGW), an annual open house for the public on the U of A campus in February, which attracted some 20,000 people. We decided to build on that too.

In VGW, we kept all the faculty open-house demonstrations and added much more. (Physics students hung a pendulum down four stories of a stairwell to demonstrate the rotation of the Earth and the hopelessness of perpetual motion.)

Radford headed a VGW Arts Festival, which included ice sculpture and a marvellous string quartet at

Convocation Hall. We spent hours designing the program, and it sold out.

And this being 1966, we organized a huge "teach-in" on Saturday and Sunday in the Education Building, with the question: "Sovereign or Satellite?" Was Canada really independent of the United States? I recall with Jeremy Wilson, on the floor of the gymnasium the night before, painting that question out on large rolls of brown paper to hang over the room.

"This Hour Has Seven Days" was the star national CBC TV public affairs program on Sunday nights. We enticed their hosts Patrick Watson and Laurier Lapierre to come to Edmonton to cover our teach-in, indeed, to be its hosts. George Grant and Mel Hurtig were among the panellists. We all watched "Sovereign or Satellite?" the following Sunday on national CBC.

**

This being 1966, my BA graduation loomed. Courses demanded attention. I was rather too busy with extracurricular stuff. I had courses in 19th Century English social history; Western Canada since 1800; a poetry course on Alexander Pope; French. As did Radford. We were not well prepared for the exams.

We met happenstance on the stairs outside Rutherford Library on a lovely May evening just before the first of our finals, looking for the same unavailable books, and quite desperate. I said, "The Sound of Music" is playing at the Varscona Theatre nearby: Let's go." We did.

The next few days were tense - three-hour exams writing essays in big halls. We'd emerge in a bit of shell-shock, wondering how we had done in obscuring our ignorance. We knew that, in many cases, we were faking it. And yet we passed.

Radford and I always annotated our BA degrees: "This course courtesy of the mercy of Brian Heeney in English social history; this of Lewis G. Thomas in the Canadian West." We earned our BA degrees for all the things we did on campus, including some academics.

***

The study season in the Rutherford Library in the spring of 1966, included something else.

In the summer of 1965, I was working in my second year at the Edmonton Tourist Bureau on the Calgary Trail. I loved it. One day in June, Bob Reece came by and said he had landed a job staffing promotional booths for the Alberta Government at state fairs in the US, as a student helper with two government staff. (The Alberta official in charge of this lived down the block from his parents.) Bob said there was a second of these promotional tours, and they were looking for another student helper. Was I interested?

Hal Martin was the guy at Alberta Industry and Tourism who managed this. I went to see him in a low building beside the Alberta Legislature. He hired me for the second tour. And in a sense, he made me.

Bob Reece and his team were assigned to Oregon and Quebec City. My team was assigned to the Canadian National Exhibition in Toronto at the end of August 1965, and the Oklahoma State Fair in latter September. I quit my summer tourist bureau job in Edmonton (too many tears), and signed on to representing Alberta "to the world."

Our per-diem in 1965 was $8.50, covering accommodation and meals. My father was travelling through Toronto that summer, and found me a room in a house not far from the CNE grounds. Arne and Irene drove me to the Edmonton airport to catch my plane – a DC8 – and standing on the terrace overlooking the tarmac (you could do so at that time), my mother asked, "Where are the engines?" She had never seen a plane up close without propellers. It was my first time on a jet.

It would be my first journey-in-air that would lead to quite another life.

***

At this point in a narrative, I am struck again by the decisive power of context in setting human fates: the nature of my parents, the circumstances of my birth, the year, the place, the times.

Just as I was developing in the womb, millions of people were dying in Nazi camps in Poland. Just as I was romping through the fields on bikes with my friends in Edmonton, millions were migrating between India and Pakistan, many to perish. Just as I was playing Tevya in high school, the tragedy of Palestine and Israel was about to break open again to no good ending. And life was continuing so beautifully for me, just carrying on, enjoying one good chance after another - maybe a bit too blissfully ignorant... but:

"Ignorance is bliss where 'tis folly to be wise." Maybe, in those early circumstances, it would have been folly to be wiser than I was: I had few fears, and fears are not always the best companions in life.

***

It was my first time away from home alone, and I was quite shocked to find myself in a rooming house in

46

Toronto. That soon eased with the opening of the CNE and the arrival of two people from the Alberta government to manage the project. I liked the CNE ambience and enjoyed the streetcar ride to the Dufferin Gate. When the CNE ended, my co-workers returned to Edmonton, and I headed to Oklahoma City to wait two weeks alone for them to return at the opening of the Oklahoma State Fair.

Those two weeks were difficult. It was 100 degrees Fahrenheit during the day. Downtown was largely deserted, though I was staying in a nice hotel. I felt entirely isolated and deeply lonely knowing that my friends were already heading back to campus at U of A. I was 20. Time crawled.

One afternoon, I walked out of downtown and found myself in a poor black community with sand roads. People sitting on stoops stared at this blonde kid, without a hat, ambling through their neighbourhood. I was entirely alone.

Perhaps I should move to the YMCA, where there would be other people I could meet. I visited there, and the vibes were unsettling for an invisible gay guy without experience. I stayed put in my hotel. One morning, I asked the manager if I could play the piano in the empty ballroom for a while, and he agreed.

At some point, I wondered if the pain of this solitude was, in fact, a kind of training for later life, where I might end up alone for long periods of time. I took it that way, and started paying attention to the dynamics of each day and my limited strategies for dealing with isolation. My colleagues finally arrived from Alberta to set up the display. But I logged that "training session on being alone" in Oklahoma City, a foreshadow perhaps of things to come.

I returned in October to the Edmonton airport at night and my friends were on that terrace throwing rolls of toilet paper down onto the tarmac as I descended the stairs from the plane (a Viscount). I was in love with being home, maybe to the point of separation anxiety with Edmonton later on.

***

In March 1966, Hal Martin asked me to come by his office to discuss the Alberta fair tours that next summer. He said Bob Reece and I had done so well the previous year as students, that each of us would lead these second tours on our own, with two other students of our choice to be part of the team. This time, my team would start in July in San Mateo (San Francisco), go to Santa Rosa in the wine country to the north, do the CNE again in Toronto, head back to the Los Angeles County Fair (Pomona) in

September, and then go on to the Dallas State Fair in Texas.

More: Canada was just one year ahead of Expo 67 in Montreal. Expo was organizing a preview of its opening this very April, 1966, featuring "Canada's Youth." Each province was to send a young man and woman to represent it at this big weekend event. Hal Martin asked if I would be the guy from Edmonton to go with the girl from Calgary to represent Alberta. Done.

So just before Radford and I met on the steps of the Rutherford Library for our final exams that May, I spent four days in Montreal, hosted and touted as a part of "Canada's youth," one year before the opening of Expo 67. Expo hostesses met us at the airport, and we billeted at great houses – me with a guy from Nova Scotia in a mansion attic in Westmount. We had a radio up there playing the Beatles from Rubber Soul " –We Can Work it Out." I listened to that song many times later, with some care.

The next three days, we were toasts of the town, touring the Expo construction site with Mayor Jean Drapeau, interviewed on TV, riding the new Metro on rubber wheels, ogling Place Ville Marie and great hotels. One night, we all went to a "disco" on Mountain Street where, for the first time in my life, I experienced people dancing in public with beers in their hands. We were indeed "Canada's youth."

I returned to the Rutherford Library at the end of April and, at coffee in the basement with Tom Radford and Bob Reece said, "We must move to Montreal and work at Expo next year. We simply must." And so we did.

***

Each year after university exams in April, we'd go camping for two weeks before starting our summer jobs. We travelled south through Montana, Idaho, Oregon, Washington and up through lush British Columbia on our way back to leafless Edmonton by late May. In spring 1966, Tom Radford came along, and we regaled him with horrifying tales of bears, snakes and spiders. His assignment was to sleep with his head near the door of the tent, with a knife by his sleeping bag. In B.C., heading for the campground at Cultass Lake, we heard on the radio that a murderer had sliced up his girlfriend in a local motel. There was an "all-watch" out for this killer, somewhere near Cultass Lake.

We made the most of it. At that campground in early May, there were perhaps three occupied sites among eighty. We were alone.

We made a big fire and left the car keys conspicuously on a piece of white paper on the hood, just in case. Who wanted to be killed for a car? Novitiate Radford slept with his head by the door, knife and axe at the ready.

Several days later, we camped at Lake Louise. In the night, a wet snowfall arrived and brought the tent down around our ears. Radford screamed " –A bear!" and reached for his knife. I felt the weight of the canvas on my head and wondered if, perhaps, this time Radford was right.

***

There was no bear: There was a wonderful coincidence waiting for me back in Edmonton.

I visited Hal Martin in his office again to review plans for the Alberta tour to fairs that summer of 1966. I had chosen my once love-interest Sheila Wynn and a fraternity brother David Bachelor to be my "employees" on this great adventure. We would start in California with a big display of illuminated Alberta photos and a working model of Alberta's topography from the mountains to the prairies under a plastic dome, rain and thunder and all.

Hal Martin and I got talking about the recent Expo weekend in Montreal for Canada's "youth." He said he

51

was the Alberta representative on the committee of four provinces responsible for the Western Canada Pavilion at Expo 67, which I had just seen under construction. He said they were having difficulty finding a manager for the pavilion. I expressed an interest. I was 20.

***

I planned to continue my studies in history – but in what field? I loved Canadian history and, especially, Western Canadian history – the province of Lewis G. Thomas (and Lewis H. Thomas in the same department). At that age, you are faced with choices that are much more profound than you know. You lack context. I was interested in the deeper history of the Canadian West, especially its embrace of multiculturalism. Absent Expo 67, I would have returned to the U of A to start grad school that fall after our second tour of state fairs.

And who knows why I persisted in my interest in that Western Canada Pavilion? Well: It was a fantastic opportunity.

THE FAIR CIRCUIT

And who knows why Hal Martin followed it up? He liked me, and there wasn't much competition.

Who can know what really happened? I met with Mr. Martin in his office again that June of 1966. I told him I needed to make commitments to the U of A by the end of June for graduate school in September. If I were to be a candidate for a position at the Western Canada Pavilion, I needed to know soon.

A week later, he asked if I could come to Montreal for a few days to meet with him and officials from the other western provinces who were responsible for the pavilion.

Soon, I was in Montreal again visiting the Expo site with the Western Canada team – senior bureaucrats from each province. We spent a good four hours touring the unfinished Western Canada Pavilion. We went for dinner. The next day we went for lunch. And then the head of the team from Manitoba asked me to go for a walk in Dominion Square, where we sat on a bench under great trees, with many people wandering by.

I thought it was just a chat. It was among the most informative and instrumental chats of my young life.

***

I cannot explain the many intersections in my experience when other people made decisions that favoured my course enormously.

I was much less the object of destructive forces than that of fine ones. Good individuals repeatedly picked me up and sent me on to greater challenges, some of which I sensed, not all of which I sought. My ambitions were almost always vague. My story resides to a great extent in guardian "daemons" hovering over my shoulder as though Hermann Hesse himself made that perfect intervention when required. Why was that?

Our flight to San Francisco landed us in time for the San Mateo County Fair. We got a motel with a pool, set up the display and spent two weeks on 10-hour duty, one of us off duty for the shift.

Two weeks later, we arrived in Santa Rosa, in the wine country north of San Francisco. We got a motel with a pool, set up the display and spent two weeks on duty, one of us off duty for the shift.

Then we headed for the Canadian National Exhibition (CNE) in Toronto (for my second time) on a big plane. They were serving Manhattans, and we had a few.

Alberta sent a duplicate of our California exhibit to Toronto to save costs. After all, we were heading back to

Los Angeles four weeks later for the Los Angeles County Fair in Pomona, and then on to Texas in the fall.

This time in Toronto, I had arranged to stay at the DU house on St. George Street, just north of Bloor. Sheila and David made other arrangements for their $8.50 a day. My room was in the attic and was hot indeed.

This was August 1966, and Yorkville was buzzing. I walked over, amazed and intimidated by the intensity of people on the street. Totally new. And who knew that Joni Mitchell et al. were in the clubs below the sidewalks?

One day, as we hung around waiting for the CNE to open and for our display crates to arrive by train from Edmonton, I went for a walk down Yonge Street to explore the city (swelled with lust as I remember). Toronto seemed an unkempt place, interesting and big, but not stylish like Montreal. Toronto had a raw vitality, though, of which I would come to know much more in later life.

**

In Dominion Square, two months earlier in Montreal, I had sat on a bench with the Chair of the Western Canada Pavilion committee. I was an improbable candidate for manager of the pavilion at 20 years of age, from Edmonton, fresh up with my BA. I had spent two days with the committee in Montreal, touring the pavilion, site and city. This was the job interview. Who knew?

If they called you at 4:30 in the morning to say that your pavilion had been flooded by a water break, how would you respond?

If one of your hostesses was arrested for prostitution and the police arrived at the pavilion, how would you respond?

If you arrived one day, and all the spruce trees growing out of the top of your pavilion roof in public sight had died, how would you respond?

If all your hostesses went on strike on a Saturday night, how would you respond?

If a visitor died of a heart attack halfway through the pavilion at noon, how would you respond?

I was unprepared for these questions and more. I answered each one as best I could. At the conclusion of our conversation on that bench, he said something like this:

"We are talking with you about this job because, despite your age, we think you can do what is expected of you. That is not the topic today. I need to assess whether you can do what is not expected of you."

At that, he got up, shook my hand, and walked away.

I thought that a brilliant moment. Whether I got the job or not, he clarified in 45 minutes to a young man that we live, always, with contingency. You cannot pretend competence without understanding that. After passing a certain grade, your test is contingency, and it is permanent, as we learn in life. The exams never end.

I walked around Dominion Square after that bench-talk, in love with the idea of Montreal and Expo 67, and hoping to be there, now more than ever. Que sera sera.

***

The CNE's opening day was approaching in Toronto, and we had no Alberta display. There was a strike involving truckers serving the railroad. Our big cache of crates was in the rail yards in downtown Toronto, but we couldn't get them out. It was two days before opening. CN Rail said I could have the crates if I got a truck to get them out. I got a newspaper.

In the classifieds, I found trucking services to rent. I called a guy and described the situation. I wanted him to break the strike, get us into the rail yard, and drive those crates to the CNE pronto. Doubling his fee did the trick.

Sheila, Dave and I met the guy at 10 PM down by the rail yards. He had an ample white truck. We drove to the depot, where a few guys were sitting at the gate with placards, preventing entry. We slowly muscled our way through them and onto the dock. We could hear them yelling for backup as CN loaded the crates. Ready to go, Sheila and Dave got in the closed back of the truck with the crates, and our driver headed for the gate. There were angry shouts and loud pounding on the side of the truck as we passed through, reverberating through the space. Then we picked up speed and 30 minutes later arrived at the CNE.

We spent all night setting up the displays, including that domed model of Alberta's landscape. A quick change back at the DU house, and I was there for opening at 10 AM, a satisfied "scab."

***

In late June, I sat in Hal Martin's office in Edmonton and said I needed to know about Expo 67. I was leaving for the summer fair circuit and needed a decision after that interview on the bench in Montreal. Two days later, he told me I was hired as Manager of the Western Canada Pavilion and would report to head office in Winnipeg on my return in October from the Texas State Fair.

I asked him later how they had the gumption to hire a guy who was just about to turn 21. He said some nice things about my performance on the Alberta tour and the interview in Dominion Square. Then he said they could not convince any appropriate person within the bureaucracies of the four Western Provinces to move to Winnipeg for a few months in winter, then on to Montreal for another eight months during Expo. People had families. The Western Canada Pavilion was stuck with me – the last option. I was not insulted.

**

We went from Toronto to the L. A. County State Fair in Pomona and didn't realize there were mountains in view of our motel until the last day, when the smog cleared. My student pals went back to university, and I went on to Dallas feeling very alone again without them.

You walked through the bow legs of a giant cowboy statue at the entrance to the Texas State Fair in Dallas. The midway was more raucous than I had seen elsewhere. One night, we were invited to an enormous ranch outside of town in a lovely gully for a BBQ, and chowed down. Then I left for Winnipeg.

**

On the roof, Western Canada Pavilion

I reported in late October to Charlie Hooey at a government building across from the Legislature in Winnipeg. Our primary task before April's opening of Expo was the hiring of 16 hostesses (no guys), four from each province, to staff the pavilion, devise their training course, select their uniforms, secure their accommodations and make various other arrangements for security and maintenance at the pavilion. I started working on a training manual that included Western

Canadian history, protocol and standards of behaviour with visitors.

Tom Radford had already moved to Montreal, seeking employment at Expo after graduation at U of A. On my frequent trips there over the winter, we ate well and plotted the coming summer. He got a job at the World Arts Festival, centred on Expo's 3,000-seat theatre. Bob Reece was completing his degree and would join us in May.

I travelled across the West interviewing candidates for hostess, most memorably in Vancouver for a week in January, where the clouds never rose higher than five stories downtown and the rain blew in sideways. We asked for bilingualism in our candidates, almost all of whom faked it adequately.

In Montreal, I roamed the streets looking for accommodation for us all. There was quite a bit available, as many landlords had evicted tenants looking to profit in 1967. Eventually, I came across 3553 Durocher, just north of Sherbrooke east of McGill University. It had sufficient apartments to be shared by our hostesses and – nirvana – an amazing two-story penthouse standing alone on the roof, a climb up some stairs from the 12th-floor elevator.

I rented the apartments for the hostesses and the penthouse for myself, Tom and Bob. It didn't strike me as odd that the building manager, who lived on the first floor, wanted to be paid in cash. That's what I did, and locked it all down.

We hired security and maintenance staff locally, monitored the construction and installation of eleven "experience capsules" ranging from a mine to a farm to an enormous BC rain forest in the middle, open to the sky with mist drifting down over a fully-loaded logging truck. That's where living spruce trees sat on boxes perched on enormous tree trunks, protruding through the top of the pavilion to the outside. (None of the trees died during Expo.) We featured no urban or cultural life in the West. Who knew we had cities?

In the midst of this, I went to Edmonton for Christmas.

***

My father was away working in the Yukon. My sister had moved out. My mother had taken in boarders for our two bedrooms upstairs – students at the university. She was working at the department store, and substitute teaching as well. She was covering her costs alone. I slept on a little bed in the basement, beside the furnace. For the first time, really, I registered how much effort my mother was making to keep things together, the rest of us blithely carrying on. I had taken our cozy home for granted, but this time, I could see her working very hard at it.

***

I looked for a place to stay in Winnipeg and found an ad in the paper to share an apartment with three guys. I went there to find they had just rented the space to someone else. They were clearly gay, and I was sad to miss the opportunity to slide into that truth.

My boss Charlie Hooey asked me home sometimes for dinner – he still lived with his mother. He had a great stereo, and I would invariably ask to hear the C-Minor organ symphony by Saint-Saens up loud – and he would oblige. He was a gentle man and gentleman, who supported my efforts in every way that memorable year.

In March, I moved to my penthouse in Montreal and primped the apartments for the hostesses. Several weeks later, I met their train at the station under the Queen Elizabeth hotel, taxis waiting to go to Durocher. Their pink uniforms and pill-box hats were waiting in the closets. Expo 67 was about to begin.

***

Montreal was gorgeous and electric with energy. The metro, with its rubber wheels and fabulous stations, took us directly to the Expo site on islands in the St. Lawrence River. Wonderful new buildings such as Place Ville Marie, the CIBC tower, the Bourse and new hotels spoke with eloquence of taste and modernity. Restaurants and clubs abounded in romantic streets adorned with flags and banners. Sleek new freeways swooped from the airport past the Expo site into the city centre. The Western Canada Pavilion had the luxury of a promotional Jeep (mine), the pavilion logo on its doors. I used it mostly to fetch friends from the airport that summer. Tom, Bob and I were effectively operating a B&B penthouse with wonderful views of the city and mountain, at the top of our game at the apex of Canada's Centennial in the prime of our youth. And we knew it.

***

Expo opened with an impressive ceremony in the Place de Nations, where I had a privileged seat as "representative of Western Canada," with my own pavilion. I hadn't realized the degree of protocol that attended such events where, suddenly, I was a minor ambassador. (Politicians and my various bosses from Western Canada made only occasional appearances in

Montreal.) I went to lunch at the Pavilon d'Honeur for a visiting prime minister and was struck that behind each of our chairs throughout the meal stood a handsome butler in white gloves to replenish glasses and remove plates. I got rather used to it, along with theatre tickets, cocktail parties and VIP tours of our pavilion itself. Indeed, just turning 22, I got used to it enough that these high trappings started fading in importance, which would have consequences for me three years on. (Your appetite for pleasure can be whetted, or sated – perhaps a dividing line among some of us.)

***

Hosting Prince Philip and Lester Pearson

Our one-room penthouse was two stories high, with glass walls facing east and west offering enormous views over Montreal, decks on either side. There was a small mezzanine at the back, where I had my bed and own bathroom up top. Radford slept underneath, and Bob had a bed tucked into an alcove in the main room, surrounded by the elevator machinery. (Bob got a job towing a Pepsi Cola ice rink around the steaming Expo site, sweaty skaters entertaining sweaty visitors in the line-ups.)

I rented an upright piano for the duration, which sat out in the open. We bought an antique dining table, and surrounded it with Paris café chairs painted in different colours. Guests slept on floor mattresses in the space between the windows and the curtains. The efficient kitchen was tucked in the back, where our cuisine of choice was steak, bought at Steinberg's. We had a decent record player and wore it out with the Beatles' revolutionary Sergeant Pepper's Lonely Hearts Club Band.

We had parties most Saturday nights, one of which ended sadly. During the party, we learned that one of our female friends from Alberta had just been killed in a car crash on the Decarie expressway in the north end of Montreal.

Some weeks later, after returning quite drunk from La Ronde – the amusement park at the east end of the Expo site – we learned of a significant war between Israel and its neighbours. We followed it closely that week. Who knew it would be the debut of a second "original sin" in Palestine?

I was at the pavilion seven days a week, for the most part, shirt, tie and jacket. We had no significant issues with the staff, though one became pregnant, I later learned. We were largely ignorant of "the news" elsewhere, occasionally dipping into the Montreal Star. The Queen, Prince Philip and Prime Minister Lester Pearson visited my pavilion on "Dominion Day," July 1, when Charlie Hooey flew in from Winnipeg to host the Queen while I took care of the Prince and PM on our tour of the building.

Charles de Gaulle came and made his famous "Vive Le Quebec Libre" call from the balcony of City Hall. I heard about his cancelled state dinner in Ottawa: A lot of great food went to the poor: perfect. Excellent sunset receptions continued onsite at Habitat, whose innovative housing units were mostly occupied by foreign delegations. The summer was a feast, not just for those of us at 3553 Durocher, but for the visitors and people of gorgeous Montreal – Canada's newly-minted "International City" – our city of the future.

But oh, how quickly that would change.

***

I was watching Walter Cronkite on the CBS evening news three years later in the basement of the Graduate College at Princeton University, where Cronkite led off with the kidnapping of the British Consul General in Montreal by the FLQ (Quebec Liberation Front). Soon, we learned of Ottawa's imposition of the War Measures Act (martial law) in Quebec and the kidnapping of its Labour Minister. Then we learned about Pierre Laporte's murder, his body found in the trunk of a car. My American fellow students looked to me for answers to this amazing story. And what were those answers?

In the summer of 1967, Montreal was at the centre of a magical year for Canada. It was our Centennial, and pageants, building projects and a train-museum crossed the country to celebrate it all. "Maitre Chez Nous" had been a slogan in the 1966 Quebec elections. Ottawa had a Commission on Bilingualism and Biculturalism" underway, and three "Wise Men" newly elected from Quebec were famously in the federal capital (Pierre Trudeau the most conspicuous). The Official Languages

Act came down in 1969, and homosexuality itself was no longer a crime (though still unacceptable and illegal in many contexts).

But the history of Quebec itself had generated, in that voluble decade of the 1960s, a passionate movement for self-respect and independence from Canada (and the Catholic church). The FLQ took a break over Expo '67, then made its move.

Three years later, Montreal was in full retreat in the face of violence, murder and "treason." I drove up from Princeton in 1971 and was amazed at the change – no change except weeds in the streets, shuttered stores and vacant lots. One great lesson I learned from Expo '67 was how contingent is the network of social relations that keeps us whole. You can descend from Montreal in 1967 to "montreal" in 1970 – in 36 months.

I was reminded of Edmund Burke, from my studies at U of A, who had cautioned against the French Revolution then, conscious of the scope for disaster in great dreams. I had two exposures to Montreal – Expo '67 and a short visit in 1971. If I wasn't already "conservative" in the sense of Burke – appreciating the value of what you have created and aware of its fragility – I was now.

To harbour perspective – to be mindful – to be careful even while brave and creative – is a condition of maturity: not easy in the face, sometimes, of passions, insecurities and dreams.

***

As we came to the closing of Expo '67 in October, all was changed. Our apartment building supervisor on Durocher claimed he had been robbed of the building's monthly cash rent in our parking garage a few weeks before. He had bruises. A few weeks later, I got a call from the police asking questions. How much did we pay in rent for all those apartments - in cash? I visited lawyers in Place Ville Marie to flesh out the story. Our apartment supervisor was charged with extortion of the building's owners and kept in jail. One day I got a call in my office from the jail, where he threatened to harm me if I testified at his trial. A few days before I returned to Alberta, I went to court and told what I knew. He stared at me with hate across the room. When I boarded the airplane for Edmonton a week later, I had a number of reasons to be happy.

One of them was "Canada: Year of the Land," the beautiful picture book of the country created for the centennial, a gift from the hostesses inscribed: "To Sir, with love" from the popular movie. We had a great staff party in the penthouse just before I left. They confided in me. I was gratified that they had concealed so much about their own adventures in Montreal: Their personal lives had been extraordinarily interesting – much more so than mine. "Get a life!" someone might have said to me had the phrase existed then.

***

I left Quebec with a sense of how different it was from Alberta – good and not so good. I loved the vaunted joie de vivre. I loved the style and robust engineering capacities demonstrated at Expo and in Montreal. I didn't like the baksheesh – the many, small bribes that came along with daily life.

I waited for an hour with a numbered slip to get my driver's license at a bureau in the city's north end without being called up, even as many other people arrived and went to the wicket. Belatedly, I noticed them slipping $20 through the wicket as they got their number. Only when I did the same was I called up.

Visiting Tom Radford earlier that year in his apartment, we returned from dinner to find the apartment robbed. I reached for the phone to call the police and he grabbed my hand to stop it: Tom had been in Montreal long enough to know that the police would find a reason to rip you off if you needed them: much cheaper to lose the stereo.

Buying the dining room table at some antique shop, I arranged delivery to our apartment on Durocher. When they arrived, they claimed the price was wrong, and said they would not unload it without another $80. Paid.

Not at Expo itself to my knowledge, but in the bones of the city, this culture of dealing offline was ubiquitous.

I had no experience of such things in Alberta – much less being threatened by my apartment manager from jail. I landed in Edmonton on October 30, 1967, late but ready for graduate school. And now, working alone to catch up in the library, the sidelined fact of being gay revived with some vengeance.

***

ALBERTA GRAD SCHOOL

Campus life had changed since my graduation 18 months earlier. The counter-culture was in swing, and the Vietnam War was gaining profile. Student groups such as the SDU were pressing for representation on faculty councils and the elimination of examinations. The university had expropriated all the houses in the adjoining Garneau neighbourhood for expansion, expelling the fraternities from their elegant old homes to reside somewhere further afield. I never saw DU again, with all its social life and connections. There was a big new Student Union Building, which I had helped to bring about. There were many more students. A gear had changed: the U of A had morphed from a community to an institution.

I had no ready links to this new reality, especially the leftist student movements that caught so much attention. I had been travelling on various forms of easy streets, immersed in other things. I had no ready view on Vietnam. And I had a compressed six months in which to study for my general exams in the MA program for history.

They gave me two big reading lists in European History and Canada. I had not yet decided where to focus.

There was one course weekly in each, otherwise I was on my own in the library. I sat on the third floor of Cameron Library (humanities) from 9 am to 10:30 pm, when I wasn't in class or walking 20 minutes home for my mother's waiting dinner. I read books and made notes. (Some young women in the humanities studied on the fifth floor – medicine- working, as we said, on their Mrs.)

At a table next to me most evenings sat a girl and guy who were obviously dating. He was enormously sexy. He was like a force field grabbing my attention and destabilizing my studies in a wonderful and disturbing way. Inevitably, he noticed my furtive glances over the winter months and would preen just a little when he got up to go wherever. This set off a serious challenge within me.

On the opposite sides of my notebook paper, I started to keep something of a diary – not a list of activities, rather thoughts on the current situation. I retain most of those diary entries made even as I sat in the library facing my nemesis.

What to do? I vowed to become a secular monk. I concluded that being gay in action was inconsistent with life in public, with career, with community, with family. So in prose and poetry, I committed myself, repeatedly in those pages, to celibacy and secrecy. That was going to be a big part of my "job" going forward, because I sensed so much potential would otherwise be lost. I had confidence that I could do this and succeeded largely for the next five eventful years.

This rooted a gap between me and other individuals at all levels of friendship, to be sure, which gap remained for the rest of my life. I tend to observe my vows, so one degree of separation from others became a secure part of my personal architecture, for good and sad.

From my Cameron library notes, January 7, 1968: "To live with what appears to be a chronic disease, to attempt to repudiate its existence every day, to wish with all your mind to be free from its shackles – this can become a heavy burden. For the effects of this ailment are not confined to its specific area of operation, but in turn, affect a whole gambit of things associated with it. Satisfaction of the disease will only feed its appetite, but its appetite must be fed. There must be some way to dampen its power, to submerge its calling needs. I wish with all my being to defeat it; my greatest desire is its extermination. The question thus resolves to my strength and in part to my audacity. I must have faith that I can win the struggle."

The "disease" was a central part of my nature and identity. I was fixed on the "extermination" of a big part of myself, the part that connects most intimately with others.

***

I ventured into two extracurricular projects back at U of A in 1967-68. My friend Marilyn Pilkington, who had worked as a hostess at the Western Canada Pavilion, ran for President of the Student Union in the spring. I served as her campaign manager, helped to organize a kick-line, and made the nomination speech for her in Convocation Hall. She won, and became the first woman to lead the U of A Student Union. (Some years later, she became Dean of Law at Osgoode Hall in Toronto and then a member of my Board of Trustees at the Royal Ontario Museum.)

My flat-mates in Montreal, Tom and Bob, decided to take that year off to travel in Europe, heading first in October to the giant anti-war/poverty protest in Washington, D.C. Happily, my friend Cam Little was still at U of A, starting first-year medicine. We hung out.

Somehow during that winter, we hatched a plan to go camping in the summer of '68 through the Soviet Union. We found a travel agency in the Ukrainian part of town, learned it was possible, marked out our route and schedule, and applied for visas. After much paperwork, the agency said we could pick up our visas at the Soviet embassy in Helsinki in June. We had a plan.

Where did this idea come from? Cam and I would spend hours together after studying. We'd speculate and imagine, and one night we came up with a camping trip through the Soviet Union. It simply had to be done.

While I lived in Montreal, my father returned from his construction projects in the North with enough money to buy the house next door to my mother's. They moved in, and my mother rented out her own house for years to come. I had a room in the largely unfinished basement, but had a bathroom and shower. And our old upright piano was down there on the concrete floor, ready and able for playing – like being five years old again.

My mother woke me each morning around 7, and produced breakfast before I headed to campus. She had dinner waiting around 6, and then I walked back to the library on campus. There was never any suggestion I should pay rent and such – it just never came up. I had a teaching assistantship at the History department, which covered tuition and paid a small stipend. I had saved money from my previous jobs.

I maintained two bank accounts – one for savings, one for spending. Each month, I allocated a certain amount to the savings account – untouchable – and deposited the rest for expenses. This habit continued throughout my life, I am gratified to say. In my highest-earning years, I saved half my after-tax income and lived below my means. Now in retirement, I spend it all at higher levels of consumption.

***

The general exams arrived in April, and I wrote essays on the history of Europe and Canada over four days. The results would not be known until June.

I gravitated to studying Europe, rather than Canada, with some gentle guidance from Prof. L. G. Thomas – the Western Canadian expert – who saw more scope in Europe perhaps. Moreover, I had stumbled over writings about the First World War, which intrigued me. By the end of the session, I was set to work with Prof. Annelise Thimme, a German with a wooden leg whose father had been the Librarian of Prussia. I now had an MA thesis to conjure up and produce. That thesis would cause ripples some 50 years later.

***

CAMPING IN THE USSR

My cousin Alan Fielding was getting married that spring of 1968 in Lausanne, Switzerland, to Valerie Noir, a young woman he had met at a religious camp in Germany sometime before. Knowing I was heading for Europe, he asked me to be best man at the wedding in May. That's where Cam and I would start our camping odyssey.

The cheapest flight to Europe for students was Icelandic Air from New York, via Rekyavik to Luxembourg. Cam's father lent us his Volkswagen beetle for the summer so we could drive across Canada to take the flight from New York. (We left the car with Cam's cousin in Nyack.) So one May morning, Cam arrived at my house to set out. My mother and father saw us off.

My father was amazed at how wide the world was at our age, compared with his in rural Alberta in the 1930s. He made one trip a year to the Exhibition in Edmonton on the train. (His mother sewed dresses for his sisters.) Otherwise the big city beyond New Norway was the town of Camrose, 15 miles away, and a bigger world existed only on the radio. He gave us a shortwave radio to keep up with the news. In the USSR, there would be no mail for two months. I said thanks, "See you in September!"

No one lives in those syncopated worlds these days. Now we live minute to minute - different creatures in many ways.

***

Cam and I spent the first night sleeping in the car somewhere in Manitoba in freezing conditions. Five days later, we were at his cousin's house in Nyack, with a day or two to explore New York City. I recall Washington Square on a Sunday filled with people in theatrical dress and, of course, the enormous scale of it all. There was no time to comprehend the social and political dynamics. We found the airport to catch Icelandic Air.

It was a four-engine turbo-prop that took eleven grinding hours overnight to reach Reykjavik. Across the aisle, two kids made out under a blanket in the dark. After breakfast at the airport in Reykjavik, the second leg of the flight was eight hours to Luxembourg, where we arrived in the evening on May 21, 1968. France was in the midst of enormous public demonstrations and strikes (a revolution?), so our train route via France to Lausanne was closed. We got tickets via Germany to Switzerland, and stopped at Aachen at midnight for passport checks by heavily medalled German officials who rather scared us in that garb. We arrived next day in Lausanne for my cousin's wedding, billeted at Tante Helene's gracious apartment overlooking Lake Geneva.

Two days of wedding celebrations were lavish, the wedding in a small, stone church down by the water. We waved off Valerie and Alan in their little Deux CV and caught a train the next day for Karlsruhe in West Germany. We needed logistics.

***

In Karlsruhe, we found a car dealership that offered for sale a dull green 1957 Volkswagen beetle with a canvas roof. I bought it with oval international license plates. We found a store that sold camping equipment, bought a pup tent, sleeping bags, pots and pans, loaded the car, found the autobahn and headed north. We would return to Edmonton four months and many adventures later.

***

We had four destinations in the Nordic countries. The first was Gothenburg, Sweden, to visit a girl Cam had met during his off-year working in Germany. We camped just outside of town and spent a fun week with Lena and her friends. Sadly, Cam and Lena could not find a night alone.

The next destination was a second cousin of mine who lived in Oslo - Torbjorn and his wife Odologue. We stayed in their gracious apartment and explored the city for a few days. (Torbjorn subsequently died young of cancer.) There was a letter from my father: I had passed my general exams for the history degree with "distinction." We learned that Robert Kennedy had been killed.

Then we headed for my Norwegian grandmother's farm in Namdalseid, north of Trondheim. We took a long route, following the coast south through Mandal, where we stole a summer's supply of toilet paper from the campground, then north, crossing fjords and snowy mountain passages on the way – a beautiful landscape in early June.

Torbjorn had drawn me a little map of how to find the farm, which we did without difficulty. They were waiting for us and put us up in a newer house down the way. We went up to the original farmhouse, where my grandmother's 91-year-old sister was still living in quarters of her own. She had photos on the mantle that included one of me and my cousins at Christmas in Camrose, many years earlier. I pointed myself out, and we hugged.

That night after dinner, my relatives took us up to a mountain lake to fish under the midnight sun. We enjoyed the trout for breakfast.

My grandmother Anna Sather saved my life while she was living on that farm in 1912. Her fiancé Sivert Westvick had left four years earlier to homestead in Saskatchewan, obtaining a quarter-section and building a small dwelling. Sivert Westvick was returning to Norway in the winter of 1912 to marry Anna Sather and bring her to Canada. We don't have her letter to him, but we have his reply: He was disappointed she had altered their travel plans to spend an extra week with relatives in the south of England on the way to North America. She had rebooked the passage, giving up their coveted place on the Titanic.

After breakfast, we bid adieu, and headed for the ferry to cross the northern Gulf of Finland on our way to Helsinki, and to the Soviet embassy to pick our visas. Pulses quickened.

***

Cam and I had one of few heated discussions on this odyssey while travelling through Norway. Observing farmers working in basic conditions along the way, I mused that there must be different qualities of happiness, and people with more education, careers, and wealth would have a higher quality of happiness than those without – more access to amazing experiences. Cam firmly disagreed, and we argued for an hour traversing the mountains. In time, I came to his side of the question, realizing that the quality of happiness falls like the gentle rain from many heavens, though with more hindsight, I realize too that not all heavens are benign. Happiness remains a puzzle.

Inevitably Cam and I launched into many such discussions. We were well-matched in our curiosity and generally made progress in exploring things together. Too, we could drive contentedly all day long without saying a word (silence, the great communion). To wit, the quality of our happiness was high, the kind aspired to by lovers, which we were not. But I did love my friend.

Our campsite in Helsinki was on the point of land by the sea just across from the city centre – a wonderfully theatrical spot. We were there for June 21 and stayed up all night for the bonfires, beer, dancing and fireworks. Light never left the sky.

We arrived at the Soviet Embassy to pick up our visas to discover they had never heard of us – our Edmonton travel agent was clearly off. Nevertheless, it was indeed possible to camp through the western part of the Soviet Union. They gave us a map showing the permitted highways and campsites. We plotted the next two months, with some arbitrary picks of locations and dates, based on distances and the little knowledge we had of the place. "Come back in five days," they said, "and pick up your visas."

We headed for Turku on the Gulf of Finland, finding a campsite by the water that included a sauna. Each evening, the Finns would get a fire roaring in the sauna, and we joined in as they threw water on the stove, creating storms of steam in that wooden box. After sweating, we ran out of the sauna and jumped into the ocean. Back on land, we flailed each other with swatches of birch branches, stimulating blood flow as they say. Then back to the sauna for round two, etc. Those nights, sleep came well and deeply. Finns are said to be among the happiest people on earth.

We were a mite surprised to find our visas actually waiting for us at the Soviet Embassy five days later - effective tomorrow. We needed to maintain our schedule in the USSR without deviation, they said, and our first stop was Leningrad the next day. Enormously excited, we arrived at the Soviet border in our little green Volkswagen with the canvas top to bemusement among the guards. They took our visas into a building and emerged 20 minutes later, shook our hands, opened the gates and welcomed us to the USSR. I watched them in the rear-view mirror as we headed down the two-lane highway toward Leningrad. They were envious.

About 45 minutes later, we were passing through a thick coniferous forest when I noticed motorcycles in the rear-view mirror. Suddenly, six or so motorcycles surrounded the car and forced us to stop. The guys examined our stuff through the windows and insisted we sell them the tent, most of our clothes and the radio on the spot. I made the point as best I could that we needed all this for our journey. No takers.

Cam and I were still in the car. I looked ahead and saw a small gap among the bikes. We decided to make a run for it, and I put that little engine into overdrive to race through. They jumped on the bikes and came up against us just as we emerged from the forest at the edge of a small village and open farmland. They fell back and I kept our speed up to its maximum of 50 miles an hour for another 30 minutes. We were in the Soviet Union!

***

Planning this whole adventure, it never occurred to us to bring a camera, and neither of us kept a diary. I thought that explicit recording of events would get in the way of memory.

***

Central Leningrad had been largely rebuilt after the horrifying Nazi siege only 25 years earlier and was lovely in many respects in that high summer light. (We were woefully unaware of the ghosts.)

After wandering the streets, with their elegant, tattered pastel-coloured buildings, our target was the Hermitage. We parked our car in the fabled, tragic square in front of the former Winter Palace and were about to head into the building when a young man approached. He was amazed that two students from Canada were starting a camping trip through the USSR in a car whose engine was in the back. Then he spied a pair of Hushpuppy desert boots in the rear window and begged us to sell them to him. We deferred, explaining that we had months to go and needed them ourselves. And in we went to the Hermitage.

We spent the whole day there, room after parquet room, struck by the grandeur of the palace (my first time in Europe) as much as the art. We had lunch in a little cafeteria – bread and sausage – and kept walking. We returned to our car around 4 pm, and there he was, the same guy wanting to buy our Hushpuppies. He had the most beautiful pleading eyes. I have always regretted that we didn't let him have them – for nothing.

***

The road to Moscow was good and our campground was in the suburbs. During five days there, we drove into town on wide boulevards with no traffic markings, every car for itself at high speed. We walked the town, toured the Kremlin and were moved to the front of the line at Lenin's mausoleum. Inside, the file moved slowly on a darkened balcony overlooking the bier, Lenin's waxy head perched at the top of what appeared to be a cylinder dressed in a suit, with two hands laid across the breast. There was an unpleasant odour in the place. I was thankful they had removed Stalin's corpse several years earlier to be buried near the Kremlin wall.

That visit was more than spooky. That night around our cook fire, we discussed how pathetic we thought it was – medieval reverence for some kind of god – in 1968! We were just getting started in the USSR, but our contempt grew over time for the communist aspects of the place, in contrast to much of the culture. We were winging it without much context, so we took lessons from our limited experiences of daily life. One thing seemed clear: This was not really a European society.

***

The next weeks we travelled the two-lane road south toward the Caucuses through Rostov, Kharkov and beyond, where I turned 23 along the way. The distances were great and our designated campground was usually a patch of ground beside a small village. There would be a little hut at the entrance, staffed by a student. He would know we were coming, take our passports and show us to our spot. He usually spoke some English or German.

We'd set up our tent, get a fire going, open one of the 50 packets of dried Knorr soup we had brought along, add some vegetables and potatoes that we bought at markets along the way, and make our lovely gruel. (I was down to 147 pounds when I returned to Alberta in September, ribs apparent.)

The student often returned with friends after dinner, approach diffidently and ask to talk. One of them was usually pretty good in English. We embraced these encounters. They were skeptical that our parents were not millionaires – that two Canadian grad students could afford to spend a summer in their own car touring Europe.

They wanted details on how we spent our lives – the nature of our accommodation, and of our universities. We would say " –Come to visit us next summer in Canada!" – and their consistent response was: "We could, but in the interest of the USSR, we will not take hard currency out of the country, which is needed to build socialism." We knew they could not leave, period. Inevitably, the talk turned to buying our jeans, shirts or shoes. We kept saying no until, one night, we sold a few things to some guys who charmed us completely.

We would show them the car with its motor in the back – none had seen a Volkswagen. We might allow them to drive it around the campsite. They often invited us back to their parents 'house – a small wooden structure, cozy on the inside, with lace curtains, icons and colourful tapestries on walls and tables. They served cucumber and tomato salad, punctuated by straight shots of vodka, sometimes washed down by beer. We tried to converse and then, late, got into the car quite drunk and found our way to the tent.

We knew we were approaching these villages from the odour of human waste spread on the fields. Near town, drunken men were often lying on the road, and an officer dressed in a grey uniform would flag us down and ask to see our papers. People emerged from everywhere, and we became skilled guides to the Volkswagen with the engine in the back. In time, we came to mock the "grey bureaucrats" who flagged us down everywhere they could to "see our papers," but we were exotic in the extreme at that time. We learned to put on a decent show. We came to understand our role.

***

We approached the Caucuses mountains across an enormous steppe on a hot July afternoon. Sunflowers commanded the view on one side of the road, corn on the other, the road lined with miles of apricot trees. Their ripe fruit had fallen into the ditches in great quantities, and we stopped to gather and enjoy. I looked up at huge cumulous clouds to the south and saw something odd: There was a bluish structure of some sort in the sky. It was the peak of a mountain whose range we would soon traverse on the "Military Road" that linked Russia with Georgia. We were headed into another culture and landscape.

***

We camped for two days at a lovely place called Ordzhonikidze (named after a founding Communist), a sylvan environment that had seen horrors during the Second World War, or Great Patriotic War, as we learned to call it in the USSR. Our campsite was beside a Konsomol youth camp, filled with teenagers sporting red bandanas around their necks. At 6 each morning, loudspeakers would blare martial music and instructions to rouse the kids. That roused us too, grumpily, but it was interesting to watch their antics and drills during the day through the fence – Boy Scouts writ large in the service of communism (Boy Scouts back home in the service of capitalism).

Our trip on the Military Road over the Caucuses to Tbilisi, Georgia, would consume a full day, we knew. We headed out early on a morning that produced desiccating heat.

It was a narrow road that sometimes broke up into gravel. High in the mountains, we encountered long, ragged tunnels usually filled with livestock seeking relief from the sun. Their shepherds seemed ancient, with linen faces and tall, thin bodies. With our canvas roof open, we put towels on our heads for protection. The landscapes were dramatic with few trees. These were the Caucuses, home to some of the longest-lived people on earth and the name of our Caucasian type of human.

By afternoon, we were heading down the other side into trees and settlements and arrived in Tbilisi around dinner. We found our campground and anticipated a good night's sleep.

Setting up the tent, I returned to the car for the poles. They were absent. In our rush to leave that morning, we had left the tent poles in the long grass of that lovely campground.

No poles, no tent. Maybe we could fashion poles from something or find new poles in town – though we knew they didn't have tents like this for sale in the USSR. We had several months to go. On the spur, we decided to drive back over the Caucuses overnight to retrieve our poles.

***

We were not permitted to drive on the highways after dark, so we approached the sentry box at dusk with some trepidation. There was the inevitable "grey bureaucrat" standing around. I asked Cam to point at something in the other direction, where I clearly cast my gaze as we sailed through, ignoring the sentry's hand signals to stop. I saw him jumping up and down in the rearview mirror and powered on, knowing he had no means of pursuit.

Thirty minutes later, a big, black Volga sedan passed us at high speed. Coming over a hill, we saw it blocking the road below. The grey bureaucrat was standing there with his gloved hand held high. He had commandeered the car to catch us.

It was tense, but a nice older couple emerged from the car, and we introduced ourselves. Feigning ignorance, we showed great contrition for not seeing the officer at the checkpoint. We described our tent and explained in sign language that we had left our poles behind in Ordzhonikidze. We laid out our papers and schedule. Then I resorted to my best card, and opened the engine in the back.

The three of them were entranced. We talked about hockey in Canada and the USSR, and I made some moves on the road pretending I had a stick. Soon, everyone was in a good mood. The people in the Volga shook our hands and resumed their journey, going ahead of us. We chatted a bit more with the officer, who indicated we could continue on. I felt a bit sad as we left him on the road in the dusk with no obvious way back to his station. Maybe he would have said yes to our journey had we asked him back there. Maybe not.

***

Tbilisi was a semi-tropical delight after weeks in Russia. Its shops were full of stuff, it had sidewalk cafes, the people were stylish, and we relaxed. I bought a wonderful vase in a shop (which I still have), a metal engraving (ditto), and we dined at a restaurant!

We had found our tent poles in the long grass in Ordzhonikidze, and made the trek back across the mountains under a star-studded night. Some 24 hours.

We spent the next four days at the beach in Sochi, on the Black Sea. Our campsite was on the ocean beside a summer holiday "resort" for Soviet families. Long, low wooden buildings provided bedrooms and communal kitchens beside a railway stop. Hundreds of Russian families were staying there, emerging onto the pebbly beach each morning beside us. Many of the older women were fat, and we watched in amazement as they picked their way into the water in their enormous bathing costumes. On Sunday, they all packed up and left. Then we heard the train, and a whole new contingent arrived for their week in the sun. It was a workers 'paradise.

Here, as in so many other places we stayed, we lined up in front of small kiosks to buy eggs or bread. The wait was often up to an hour, arriving at a single wicket that sold either eggs or bread (that was another line). Often, the wicket closed before we got there, out of food. When we did get there, we learned that one egg might cost 10 kopecks, the second 20 kopecks and the third (if allowed) 40 kopecks. They had a market system, after all! The bread kiosk was simpler: one loaf of one kind of bread, period.

We bought our vegetables from well-stocked open markets, run by farmers themselves. Once in a while, we visited a special food store reserved for party members that accepted only US dollars as currency to buy some chicken or meat. The conspicuous limitations of the system were part of everybody's day.

***

It was time to continue on our schedule. We headed north up the lovely Black Sea coast and then inland to retrace our steps to Kharkov, where we would turn west into Ukraine. August was upon us, and we had miles to go.

Soviet gas stations were fun. This is where we encountered the ebullience of Russians, shouting, laughing, cajoling around the pumps. Of course, our arrival torqued the scene, what with our engine in the back and all. We looked forward to gassing up in this fiesta atmosphere.

Coming back into Russia from Georgia at one such station, I thought it prudent to change the oil in our car. They drained the crankcase and started pouring oil into the top of the engine. The oil looked rather dark.

We could make our designated campsite at Kharkov that evening, except the engine in our car soon jolted to a stop at the bottom of a long hill. Dead. A trucker towed us back into the town of Slavyansk, where there was a gas station and garage at the edge of town. We set up our tent in a cornfield behind the garage, and they started working on a car they had never seen before.

It was unusual to eat our meals in the little restaurant attached to the garage – we always ate "at home" around the fire. The food was basic, and their version of soda-pop was a bottle of flat, sugared water that came in various pale colours but always tasted the same. I said to Cam that we could make a fortune with a Pepsi franchise in Russia but, of course, that was illegal. By this time in the trip, we were fully aware of the limits built into their economy, though their experience was one of constant improvement since the war. I was a conscious capitalist now for sure.

The next morning, they started dismantling our engine. They took each piece as it came off and put it on a ledge going around the room in the order that it arrived. They got down to the pistons and discovered a blackened valve that had blown apart. What now?

They explained it and showed a similar valve from a Soviet Lada car. That valve was bigger than ours. For the next day, they ground and reshaped that valve to approximate a Volkswagen's. On the third day, they started putting the engine back together in the order they had taken it apart.

That afternoon, a crowd gathered to witness the result. A mechanic got into the car – and it started, with plumes of black smoke spewing from the tailpipe. Applause abounded. Then, everyone had their turn at driving it around the area, as we gathered our tent and such to leave. I asked how many rubles I owed for the miracle they had just performed.

It would be 65 rubles, but they didn't want rubles. (What of real desire could rubles buy them?) They wanted our tent in payment, which had been standing so smartly in that cornfield. I explained that we had many weeks of travel ahead and could not spare the tent. OK, they said, how about that shortwave radio they had seen in the restaurant?

I conferred with Cam. We said maybe, but the radio was worth 100 rubles, and they should know that it had batteries they would find hard to replace. "No problem." I gave them the radio, they gave us 35 rubles, and we hit the road for the campground in Kharkov (which our mechanics had called to explain we would be three days late).

Part way up the highway, we started feeling nauseous. Fumes from the engine were leaking up into the car. We pulled back the roof and opened the windows, and that is how we travelled for the next six weeks, rain or shine: The wind became our tailpipe.

***

I am grateful that our engine conked out and that we spent three days in Slavyansk. We got to know the local people a bit, joke with them, drink with them, haggle with them. They were wonderful souls, intelligent, skilled and generous, inventive and kind. Cam and I discussed this, distinguishing between cultures and regimes, communities and ideologies. The state could be a rogue distinct from the people. (Slavyansk showed up in the news some 45 years later as one of the battlegrounds between Russia and Ukraine after the "Maiden Revolution.") The USSR was not a European country, rather a complex cousin.

***

The drive across the steppes toward Kiev was marvellous, sunflowers to the horizon, corn and wheat bending in the wind. Large billboards showed enthusiastic young farmers with raised fists vowing to meet quotas on eggs and grains. It was clear and hot when I noticed a huge grey truck looming in the rearview mirror. It honked its horn and we pulled to the side.

99

We waited there for some 45 minutes as a cavalcade of military vehicles lumbered past, heading west. Only when we left the USSR weeks later did we learn they were heading to crush the "Prague Spring" in Czechoslovakia. We had unknowingly pulled up the rear.

Our campground was in a forest on the outskirts of Kiev, an impressive city by all appearances despite its horrors during the Great Patriotic War. With our "radio money" we splurged for dinner at the big hotel on the hill, a red star on its peak. The dining room had two old refrigerators sitting out among the tables in a large, elegant space. The menu was long, and we chose carefully. The waiter then informed us that only three things on the menu were available. I chose the cutlet with green peas that came floating in a sauce of fat. The beers helped.

***

Our spirits were high as we awoke to our last day in the Soviet Union and headed for the Hungarian border, where we would go to Budapest and then on to Vienna. We were tired of communist culture, though not the Russian one. We were, in fact, contemptuous of it. Time to leave.

At the border, Hungarian officers checked our passports and noticed we had grown beards during our six weeks of camping in the USSR. Those beards would have to come off – there was a hut over there to do the shaving. We objected, saying it was clear from our documents that we had been travelling in the USSR, and that we were who we were. "Shave off the beards," they said.

Cam and I conferred. By this time, as I have said, our patience for grey bureaucrats and petty intrusions was spent. A little crowd of travellers had gathered. I returned to the officers and said, "I will travel a thousand kilometres before I will enter Hungary at the price of shaving my beard." The crowd broke into applause, and we got in the car and headed back into Ukraine. A few kilometres in, we took out the map and decided to try Romania, just to the south.

***

Unlike Hungary, there was a big Soviet border installation at the Romanian frontier. Officers demanded we take everything from the car and lay it out on the grass. Then they asked us to bring every scrap of paper we had into their office, plus all our money. They counted the money looking for evidence that we had been trading on the black market. We had a few too many rubles from selling clothes and the radio, but not enough to matter. The problem came with the map.

I still had the hand-drawn map my cousin made in Oslo, showing the way to the family farm in Namdalseid. They suspected it described some secret place in the USSR. I forget how we convinced them otherwise, but they relented.

Meanwhile, they had the car over an open pit, checking the undercarriage and running wires around the wheels. Eventually, they said we could pack up again. We were about to leave when a beautifully-dressed officer – rich blue uniform and white gloves – appeared and asked in warm terms how our trip had been in the USSR. Of course, we loved everything about it. Tell your friends, he said, and saluted us on.

The actual border was several hundred metres away. We proceeded down a steep incline where wet logs lay across a little stream, then gingerly up a muddy track to the border itself – large steel gates joined at the centre. A minute later, the gates started opening with a loud buzz. As we passed into Romania, I touched the passport in my pocket and said to Cam: "But for this, we would be eternally prisoners in that lovely and horrible place."

About two kilometres into Romania, a young man wearing white overalls flagged us down. He asked how long we had been in the USSR, and shook his head in disbelief. He had a big canister and a pump with nozzle, and explained that he had to disinfect the whole underside of our car against various diseases we probably picked up there. "They are dirty," he said in disgust. Purified, we headed into the Balkans.

It took several days to circumvent Hungary through Romania and Yugoslavia, which impressed us with their well-stocked stores and relaxed ambience. Arriving in Austria from the south, we were struck again by the wealth and thrived on jaeger-schnitzels in mushroom gravy. Vienna was heavenly, with a letter from home at American Express. Now it was on to Cologne, Germany, where Cam had friends and we would sell our beloved car. Except...

***

We arrived at the German border, when real borders still existed in Europe, showed our documents and prepared to move on. "Just a minute," said the guard, who came out of his sentry box. He walked around the car, examining. "Your tires are bald and you will need to buy new ones before you can enter Germany." I explained that we were selling the car in three days and didn't have money for new tires. No go.

So we turned around, got out the map and looked for another border entry further east. We arrived at a second crossing, and the same thing happened. (The Germans are quite methodical.) This time, however, the guard said there was an auto shop three kilometres ahead on the highway within Germany, he would call them to say we were coming, and we could get our new tires there. "Perfect" I replied.

We took the first exit, plunging into the countryside as fugitives from the law. (I wondered if that guard was just letting us go.) We would drive to Cologne only on back roads in the next few days to avoid police. Meanwhile, where were we?

We settled on Passau as our first night stop, a town at the confluence of the Danube, Inn and Ilse rivers, the Inn being the border with Austria. We were enchanted. The campground was within the walls of an ancient castle high on a cliff overlooking the town, where an enormous church projected above the intriguing warren of its medieval streets. We had dinner at a restaurant up there, and I vowed to return someday.

If our tires had not been bald, we would not have known Passau, and I would not have lived there the following summer.

***

We stayed in Cologne with Cam's friends and slept in beds for the first time in months. It felt strange to be up in the air, precarious even. We drove to the VW dealership the next day to sell the car. They didn't want it: It was useless by now, they said. I couldn't leave it on the street. They graciously took it off my hands for $50.

***

We took a train to London to catch an actual KLM jet for New York in a few days to pick up the other VW and return to Alberta. We shaved off our beards, and I was struck by how young and handsome Cam was. We took our bags and tent to Victoria Station, where we could check in one day early for the flight. The baggage was substantially overweight, the tent the costly culprit. We couldn't afford to bring it back for the last leg of our journey. We checked the other stuff and left with the tent. What to do with it?

"Let's watch it get stolen," I said. We were in busy Victoria Station, surely filled with pickpockets and thieves. We leaned the tent against a wall near the entrance and moved away to observe the scene. Within moments, a guy wandered up and stood beside it, casually looking around. Five minutes later, he scooped it up and hastened out to our muted applause.

We picked up Cam's VW in Nyack, N.Y. and headed west in the middle of September, without our tent. We slept in the chilly car, which was much more powerful than the one we had left behind. We had a hamburger at a gas station in Lloydminster the evening of our arrival in Alberta. I knocked on my parents 'door around 10 pm and slept again in a bed, up in the air. The next day, I went to the university to start my thesis year for the MA.

My souvenirs of the trip consisted of that vase and metal drawing from Tblisi, a bunch of prints and posters from the USSR, and a Moroccan camel-leather footstool that I unaccountably bought in Cologne. The prints and posters became dispersed (I left all the good posters in the history department at U of A), but I still have the vase, the metal drawing and the footstool. Miss the posters.

***

That camping trip shaped me in predictable ways. I could take care of myself in unusual situations, now with more confidence. I had a richer sense of architecture and the variability of ancient cultures. I had stronger opinions on the failings of communism and the profound risks of prescriptive ideology. I had more patience for periods of boredom, rainy days in the tent, too many days in one place. My trust grew in people on the street, who so often came to our aid. Except, on the return to

Edmonton, I missed Cam terribly as we both went back to school.

I spent two summers travelling the fair circuit for Alberta in 1965 and 1966, a year at Expo 67 in Montreal, a full summer camping in Europe in 1968. I lived worlds apart from the fluid summers of love among my peers and the awakening of their social views and politics. I was a blithe spirit in voluble times.

***

A MASTERS THESIS + FILM FRONTIERS

On my return to Edmonton, I traded in my 1957 Pontiac on a used, shimmering 1966 black Volvo coupe, with red bucket seats. It has always been among my favourite cars – for which I have a weakness.

Back in the history department, I was teaching assistant to Annelise Thimme, who taught a survey course in European history. I occasionally taught the course, bringing Wagner records to class to illustrate themes in the 19th Century. (The students kept asking, "When do we get to Hitler?") But my big task was to choose and produce a thesis for my Master's degree.

I had run across writings of Bertrand Russell, Romain Rolland and Sigmund Freud in the previous year's reading lists. They all had something unusual to say about the First World War as they experienced it. I thought it would be interesting to go deeper, compare and contrast and see what we could learn from their writings at the time, sometimes to each other.

I proposed this to Annelise, and she agreed. That's all she really did. She didn't assign additional readings or give anything more than editorial feedback when I started submitting material to her. I was doing this pretty well on my own.

She did, however, say that I would need German to advance at the Ph.D. level, and she was committed to me studying with her famous friend Karl Schorske in the history department at Princeton. Thus, I enrolled in first-level German, held at 8 am Monday through Friday in the basement of the Arts building. I left my house at 7:30 am, walking through the winter darkness, and emerged from German class at nine into a grey, frigid dawn, soon leavened by coffee and cinnamon rolls at the Tuck Shop.

I spent most of that year in the library, back at the table on the third floor. The handsome guy sitting across the way with his girlfriend was back, reproducing the exquisite torture I had known the year before. Fervent diary entries in my notebooks grew. An attractive girl invited me to her fraternity formal, where I did not kiss her goodnight. She left a brown paper bag on my library table two days later: Inside was Eric Fromm's book The Art of Loving.

Meanwhile, Tom Radford had returned to the history department to work on his own degree. We had adjacent offices, and hung out constantly. One day, strolling along Saskatchewan Drive, Tom admitted to deep boredom with academia, and we recalled our days of competing "film companies" as undergraduates. This time, we decided to create a real one, to make documentaries about anything that mattered, while continuing with our studies.

We came up with the name "Film Frontiers" and visited a print shop on Jasper Avenue to make up business cards. We created a design in two colours and used Tom's parents 'apartment as the address. Film Frontiers was born.

We had never made a serious film. We didn't have a camera or any other equipment. But we shopped ourselves around as new-wave, vigorous documentary filmmakers in Alberta, 1969. The guy heading the university's media office suggested we were "used car salesmen" after we pitched him with a script. Okay, okay. But we were lucky to discover a newly-created provincial educational television authority in Edmonton (MEETA), open to proposals. We pitched a script focused on a student's transition from high school to university – what it entailed and how to handle it. They accepted it and we settled on something like $200 for a 20-minute film that Tom and I would introduce and discuss in a CBC studio. Nirvana!

We found a guy in the Yellow Pages who advertised himself as a cameraman. We hired Jim Tuskin and his 35 mm camera to do the shoot, watching his every move along the way. Tom peered over his shoulders as he edited the film at his studio. We hosted the film sitting on stools at the CBC, with some additional discussion, and MEETA was pleased. There would be more work with them soon.

So was born what became "Filmwest Associates" two years later, involving a larger group of friends. Tom left academia for film full time, and Filmwest produced several of Western Canada's leading writers, directors, editors and cinematographers in subsequent decades, including Anne Wheeler and P. J. Reece. By the mid-1970s, Filmwest had morphed into the first Alberta office of the National Film Board, headed by Tom Radford. Bored grad students can generate surprises, as we have seen many times.

**

I read a newspaper story in January 1969 about Canada's participation in Expo '70, to be held in Osaka, Japan, only three years after the Montreal World's Fair. On a whim, I sent a letter to their office in Ottawa, describing my experience at Expo '67 and indicating an interest in Expo '70. Without so much as a phone call, I received a letter offering me the position of Visits Officer at the Canadian Pavilion, starting in January 1970 in Osaka. In effect, I would be the head of protocol for Canada at the World's Fair. My Master's thesis would be done by then, and I would take a year off before my Ph.D. at Princeton to work in Japan. Why not?

***

My focus, meanwhile, was on the thesis, which I was enjoying immensely. One book, diary and manuscript led to another, enriching the narrative about the purported causes and nature of the First World War. Bertrand Russell was a revelation, and I needed to read a wide variety of Freud's work to put his views in context. I came to hold Romain Rolland in some contempt for his naivete, but he represented a relevant idealistic swath of European culture and opinion. I fed each chapter to Annelise, who would make notes in the margins. By spring, I knew I would need the fall semester to complete the thesis before my departure for Japan. Besides, my German language skills demanded more serious attention.

The Goethe Institute offered summer immersion courses in Germany, and I decided to take one – but where? Passau came to mind – that lovely "bald-tire" town on the Danube just across the River Inn from Austria where I had camped the year before. Happily, Goethe Institute had a school there, and I got a place for July and August. I would live with the family Peter in the old town centre, my bedroom window looking directly down onto the Danube behind. And after seven months of daily study in Edmonton, I would learn German rather well that summer.

***

In the spring of 1968, we all went to see Stanley Kubrick's film, 2001. It was a marvel, of course, but the last scene stopped me in my tracks. The character played by Kier Dullea arrives beyond space and time in a conventional-looking room you might find on Earth. He is entirely alone in the universe, though food somehow appears on the table, where he clinks his cutlery. Ultimately, he is very old and dying on his solitary bed, breathing noisily. I saw that immediately as my fate in the end: alone in some nice room, clinking cutlery and waiting (for rebirth a la Kubrick?). I have watched that scene many times since, also recalling my solitary weeks in Oklahoma City, and it still resonates.

***

I almost died in Passau. The day I registered at the Goethe Institute, I met a handsome fellow student from the USA. He was on his way to buy a kayak and head out onto the Inn river, which met the Danube at Passau's point. I accompanied him. He bought the one-man kayak and then invited me to come along for his first foray. A non-swimmer, I slipped into and under the front, with his legs around me, and we headed out.

The Inn is a large, fast-flowing river with a lot of barge traffic. We got out into the middle, a barge came by, and its wake flipped us over. I remember being underwater, unable to extricate my legs from the front of the kayak. Somehow, he pulled me out, and we surfaced. He had the rope of the half-submerged kayak in his hand, and I grabbed it. He was a powerful swimmer and headed for the bank along the German side of the river as we sped down toward the confluence with the Danube. I could see people running along the pedestrian walkway to keep up with us. We got close enough that they could reach us with long poles that hung from the walls for just this kind of occasion. They pulled us in. I vomited on the concourse and felt my wallet still in my back pocket. I walked home soaking wet to the disconcertion of the family Peter and thanked the gods.

***

The Goethe Institute was housed in an old mansion on a hill overlooking the Inn river and town. I walked up a steep path through the woods to arrive in time for a continental breakfast on the lawn with my peers. Classes went from 8 am to noon, and then from 4 pm to 6, and included speech labs and lots of grammar. We did not eat with our host families except at Sunday brunch. We had restaurant chits for lunches and dinners at certain pubs around town. Soon, we settled into amenable cliques, mine including no Americans and informally led by a wonderful guy from Spain - Francisco. Our only common language in that group of six or so was German, and we spent every lunch and dinner together. One night in early August in our favourite Gasthaus, we got into a passionate debate about something that went on and on. Then Francoise from France noted we were no longer translating – we were speaking German straight-up. We had passed through a gate. More great German beer!

One weekend, the Institute organized a trip to Prague, a couple of hours away on a bus. It was the first anniversary of the Soviet invasion, to which, unknowingly, I had pulled up the rear in Ukraine one year earlier. There were posters everywhere protesting the Soviet presence. I had unusual context for that weekend.

Near my last day in Passau, I went for lunch in a restaurant where everyone sat at long communal tables. I fell into conversation with a German couple and their two kids. At some point, the guy asked me, "Are you from Hamburg?" I was thrilled.

***

In September, I was back in the history department, typing up my thesis, with all its footnotes and bibliography. Annelise seemed pleased, and it was time to submit my formal application to Princeton, where Prof. Schorske would be expecting me one year later, after my time in Japan. There was an asterisk in the form that said a certain requirement was necessary except for applicants to the Woodrow Wilson School of Public and International Affairs. I flipped to the back of the Princeton catalogue and read all about it. It was clear to me that I would much rather continue my studies at the WWS rather than in history. I loved history but realized I didn't want a career in it.

I scratched out the history on the form and inserted WWS. I wrote the requested essay on some public policy questions, explained why I lacked pre-requisite courses in economics and statistics, and wrote another essay on why I would not be submitting SAT scores. I informed Annelise of this change of mind, and she threw me out of her office in a rage, saying she would withhold her letter of recommendation to Princeton. A week later, she relented, and off went my application, quite doomed, I was sure. No more need for German, however, whatever happened at the WWS.

The time came for my thesis defence before Annelise and two other professors. The outside examiners asked broad questions about the nature of European society in the late 19th Century, for which I was not well prepared. The session concluded rather quickly. The next day, Annelise said they liked the thesis but wanted it reorganized into biographical chapters rather than my thematic ones. I found that strange, and said sure. I submitted the revised text after my return from Japan and got the MA in 1971.

(The subjects of the thesis, expanded by me in a lecture for the Munk School at the University of Toronto in 2014, probed the "collective unconscious" as a fundamental root of the First World War: not railway schedules or bad communications or the egos of certain emperors. Many people alive then opined that Europeans were hankering for a "great war" to clear the air of decadence and boredom, to find adventure, to "live again" by dying meaningfully. References to the power of the collective unconscious were largely sidelined then and, at my Munk lecture, generated conspicuous resistance – not to mention anxiety bordering on hostility. It is one of the more important, unexplored and repressed subjects in historiography.)

***

Canadian Pavilion, Expo 70

A red diplomatic passport came in the mail, and I set off for Japan the first week of January 1970. First stop was Honolulu, where I found myself in a pink hotel, the sound of waves breaking on the beach below my window. The flight to Tokyo was 11 hours, and I recall excellent Japanese food. Arriving in Tokyo with my granny glasses, long hair and leather jacket, I was directed to the diplomatic line, where a guy from the Canadian embassy was waiting. We went to a luxury hotel where I would stay for a week of orientation before heading to Osaka.

The embassy was a lovely mansion set in spacious grounds across from the Imperial Palace. (A new embassy building is now part of the site, where I hosted a reception for the ROM almost 40 years later.) Among briefings and dinners, my guy took me to a bathhouse in the red light district under an elevated railway. Two young women took us to separate rooms for a massage, etc. I indicated to her that I didn't want sex, so she put me into a deep little tub of very hot water and closed the top around my neck. I was about to pass out when she liberated me and sent me back downstairs. The next day, I was on the bullet train for Osaka.

***

The Expo '70 site was on Osaka's outskirts in the hills. They built an apartment community nearby to house foreign staff. I was in Building C26, on the fourth floor, which would ultimately become home to local people. It had a little kitchen and a living room that doubled as the bedroom when you rolled out a futon on the tatami mats in the evening. The bathroom had a toilet with a big poster above with drawings in Japanese, instructing people how to use it. There was a small balcony and food market across the way. We were one stop by train from the Expo site. This was home for the duration.

One day early on, I took the train to downtown Osaka on a Sunday afternoon to check it out. On return to the enormous train station, with no signs in English, I realized I didn't know the name of my destination. Kind people started gathering around me, and I said Expo, Expo, Expo! They led me to the right train.

If you are fortunate to have one, know the name of your home.

***

Canada had the Number One protocol position at Expo '70, after hosting the previous Class A World Exposition in Montreal. We also had the most lavish pavilion, designed by Massey-Erickson, an enormous truncated pyramid covered in mirrors surrounding an open-air courtyard with a sunken pool and performing stage. The exhibits were housed on three sides of the pyramid, connected underground beneath the four open apertures at the corners. Giant glass and plastic "flowers" grew up from the pool to the open sky. It was marvellous architecture.

Our executive offices and VIP facilities were on the second floor on one side, with unbroken windows gazing down on the courtyard below. The schema was white, silver and wood – white carpets, lamps and furniture, Lucite tables and silver accents, all under a dramatic sloping roof of B.C. fir beams. My office was part of this schema – my "desk" folding down from the wall in what was otherwise a salon.

It was only January, but we had a management meeting every morning at 10 am in Commissioner-General Patrick Reid's office. We were all just getting to know each other, and on the third day, Patrick asked me to hang back. In my years at the University of Alberta, I was known primarily as Thor rather than Bill Thorsell. In Osaka, I reverted to Bill Thorsell. Patrick was from Ireland. He said he rather disliked the name Bill and asked if he could call me William – my actual birth name. Certainly, I replied, as I had left Bill behind some years ago in any case. Thus, I became William for the rest of my life.

I quickly embraced Patrick Reid as a mentor – a sophisticated, energetic, generous man who had brought his wife and two children with him to Osaka (his daughter married Rick Hansen). He became one of the role models in my career.

(Names: When I came to Toronto, a number of people reverted to calling me "Bill" when I introduced myself as William. I would gently correct them, and some of them would carry on with Bill – the diminutive.)

***

Before Expo opened, I made plans on how to host VIPS, lunches and dinner parties in our beautiful suite. (The transparent Lucite dining table could seat 22.) I met with our chef from Ottawa about the larder in the basement – vast quantities of Alberta beef, Arctic Char, Salmon, duck, blueberries and beer. Oh, and yes, Canadian wine. We held a number of early lunches and dinners for officials from other pavilions to get our pattern down. And then, as Number One in the protocol, Patrick Reid would host a special reception for all other commissioners general a few days before Expo's opening in mid-March – my first crisis.

I was in charge of sending the invitations, among other things, for that inaugural evening. Everything was in train for a lavish launch.

One Saturday morning, some weeks out from the reception, I got a call at home from Patrick's secretary asking that I come to the pavilion immediately. I jumped the train and arrived at a full-court press of the management group waiting in his office. There had been a disaster.

The commissioner-general of the British pavilion was Sir John Figges. In addressing the invitation to our reception, we had inscribed the envelope to "Sir John

Figges and Mrs. Figges," rather than Lady Figges. He had called Patrick in outrage and threatened to turn down the invitation. Patrick stood glowering at me, looking for a response, surrounded by other management types, some of whom clearly resented my Albertan youth and insouciance from the outset.

I was shocked by the menial nature of this "crisis" and unaware of the breach in protocol. It seemed quite ridiculous on the face of it. But I made a decision on the spot to embrace the mistake.

I said it was my job to conduct protocol for Canada at Expo, and this had been an egregious error. No one else was responsible, and I asserted that our quality control in protocol would change to see that no such incidents happened again. I apologized to everyone involved.

Patrick's face lit up; other faces fell. He shook my hand and expressed confidence in our future. He pressed a little button on the wall beside his desk (I had one too), and a waiter appeared. Gin and tonics all around, he said, just before noon.

I wasn't glib in saying what I did. Two lessons had been driven home: Double-check your conspicuous work, and never evade responsibility for your commitments. After that morning, I could feel that Patrick Reid's trust in me was solid. It would need to be.

***

I met my Japanese assistant every morning to review the list of VIPs coming that day and weeks ahead. We had five ranks, ranging from simple access to exhibits through the VIP entrance to heads of state. People in the middle would get a greeting upstairs with me or the commissioner-general, maybe tea or a drink, sometimes a little gift, before heading through the exhibits with a guide. We soon had it down to a sociological science on how to discriminate well. Ultimately, three visits stood out: The Emperor of Japan, the prime minister of Canada, and Marlon Brando.

***

The pavilion was staffed by Canadians in their twenties who could speak Japanese. We had a resident dance company for the stage – Feux Follets from Montreal - and the rock band Chilliwack from B.C. Many of the guides and support staff lived in my building, and we soon got to making dinners together on our tatami mats – Shabu Shabu was the favourite, rare slices of beef and vegetables on a hot frying pan. Community blossomed.

Louise was a senior secretary from Quebec, tall blonde, well-endowed and a ton of fun. We took the train to Osaka on rare days off to wander the intriguing narrow streets. Japanese men on the train were dumbstruck by Louise's fulsome breasts, barely contained in her tank-top. She enjoyed turning around suddenly to catch them off-guard. Guys would run ahead of us in the narrow streets to alert shopkeepers that we were approaching, so it was something like a parade to walk with Louise through those delightful alleyways. She had a great sense of humour and pride about her power over men, distinct perhaps from the current age.

In early June, Patrick and I examined our stock of food and libations. We had far too much Canadian beer, so Saturday nights after Expo's closing, we hosted site-wide beer parties in our courtyard for everybody's staff, very well-attended. Many Japanese have a low tolerance for alcohol, and some were falling into the pond in high spirits. The fiestas continued, with our security guys patrolling the pond to prevent inconvenient drownings.

***

Opening weekend was all protocol and parties, with Canada front-and-centre. Canadian media arrived and joined a liquid reception upstairs. As the evening drew to a close, I heard a noise from the VIP entrance at the bottom of the stairs. Staff rushed up and led me down to where CTV National News Anchor Harvey Kirk was lying on the floor with some blood on his face, having crashed inebriated through the glass-top reception table in the middle of the room.

The first rule in a protocol is "nothing awful ever happens." I requisitioned the pavilion's golf cart immediately, into which Mr. Kirk was loaded on his way to the train. We pitched in to clean up the glass and shuffle it into a corner. Guests began coming down the stairs to leave, escorted by Patrick Reid, who asked, "Something up, William?" Staff blocked a view of the table: "Nothing," I said with a smile.

***

Emperor Hirohito planned a protocol visit to Expo, and, given our Number One protocol priority, he would visit only the Canadian Pavilion as a form of visiting them all. I spent many weeks meeting with the Imperial Household planning this event, which would be the first time that a Japanese Emperor had left his "sovereign territory" to step on foreign territory – Canada's pavilion was technically Canadian soil.

Weeks ahead, a small man about the size of the Emperor came with officials, and we walked through the pavilion visit from beginning to end, Hirohito's stand-in shuffling along in the manner of the Emperor so we could gauge speed, stairs, ramps and such. We did this several times. Ultimately, the Emperor arrived at a full-court press of Mounties on horseback at the entrance, silver-suited guides in formation and Patrick Reid in full form at his height exceeding six feet, with his wife Alison in splendid attire. It went off perfectly to great Japanese press attention. At his office later, Patrick pushed the button on the wall: "Gin and tonics all around."

(My handsome Japanese waiter brought me a gin and tonic every afternoon at 4, as a matter of course. This was the diplomatic corps, after all.)

***

Every country had a "national day" at Expo '70, celebrated with official visits. Alone among pavilions, we had a second large flagpole and would raise the flag of that day's honoree nation beside our own as a salute to our colleagues. One day, Patrick Reid asked our PR guy if anyone else knew we were doing this. Had there been any notice? There had not: It was a "worthwhile Canadian initiative," invisible.

Reid flushed and asserted that good deeds such as this did not exist without public notice – They Did Not Exist! Within a few days, there were stories in all the Japanese newspapers about this "worthwhile Canadian initiative."

So this was another tangential learning from Japan: Strategy requires good thinking and good deeds, and much of that is wasted without a profile. Marketing is core to achievement, including good deeds. (Today, many consultants focus on managing the consequences of bad deeds alone, leaving a productive part of the field empty.)

***

Canada's National Day was in May, coinciding with Prime Minister Pierre Trudeau's visit to Australia and Asia, the last stop on his way home. It meant something of an extravaganza. The entire RCMP Musical Ride, including horses, flew over the pole to perform in the main plaza, covered in soil for the day. We brought the musical "Ann of Green Gables" to the large Expo Theatre (Ann being very popular in Japan). And we organized an enormous after-party for all the theatre guests at the Japanese "Guest House" where Canadian food and two Canadian bands would show off our many cultural attributes. (Doing the seating plan around Trudeau's theatre box took a month of back-and-forth with players in his office).

Trudeau would be with us for three days, and I worked through the spring with Patrick Reid, the PMO and Japanese protocol to set the agenda. It was complex and ambitious and destined for big trouble indeed.

The governor of Osaka Prefecture held a "State Dinner" downtown for Trudeau on the first evening, which would culminate on our National Day two days later. During the meal, Trudeau took the schedule we had printed up out of his pocket, reviewing it. Patrick Reid saw him fussing. In the end, Trudeau gave him the schedule with just about everything crossed out, preserving the morning event in the Plaza and the after-party in the Guest House. (He said he was tired at the end of his trip.)

The day following was fully scheduled with official pavilion visits – Japan, Great Britain, France, USA etc., lunch at our pavilion, and private dinner downtown. "He can't do this," I said. Patrick raised his eyebrows and looked at me with a dollop of pity. So how would Trudeau spend the next day, I asked? Patrick said Trudeau wanted to visit the site incognito, which meant only with his RCMP protector and me. Incognito.

We cancelled all the visits. I met Trudeau at our pavilion in the morning, and we headed off on foot visiting. He asked many questions about my past and my job as we wandered through the crowds. "Let's start with Britain," I said.

I knew all the protocol people at Expo by then, and we arrived at the simple VIP entrance for Britain unannounced. I told my colleague there that his official visit was cancelled. Trudeau wanted to go through the pavilion incognito with me and not make a fuss. About half-way through, there was a commotion, and Sir John Figges rushed up to join us. Trudeau was tolerant and not pleased. Sir. John was incandescent, and Lady Figges was nowhere to be seen.

And so went the day: We visited most of the pavilions on Trudeau's cancelled schedule incognito until the word got around, and then we were swamped halfway through only to wander lonely as a cloud back into the crowds. He loved going incognito, and we had a pretty good time. Lunch was out of bento boxes purchased from a kiosk.

After big ceremonies on the Plaza the next morning, Trudeau went to Kyoto to visit the temples. I met up with him again around 7 pm, as all those guests were filing into the Expo Theatre for Ann of Green Gables. Trudeau's box included the Reids and the Ambassador of Japan and his wife – sans Trudeau. I had the pavilion's golf cart, and Trudeau and I scooted around until we found a little Korean restaurant. We discussed the Japanese way of being, the nature of these expos – sitting on the floor savouring Korean delights and some quantity of sake. Around nine, I said Ann of Green Gables was ending, and we should make our way over to the big after-party in the Guest House.

We pulled up in the golf cart as most people were arriving from the theatre. Patrick Reid and Alison were waiting at the portal sporting great smiles and took him off my hands into the swelling congregation. I followed some minutes later and marvelled at the grandeur of the place, the enormous crowd, tables laden with Canadian beef, fish and fruits, bars everywhere. At the far end, there was a "big band" playing the classics; far around a corner was our Canadian rock band belting it out. I relaxed and settled in for a good time.

Then came a tap on my shoulder. A Japanese official said the Japanese Ambassador to Expo wished to speak with me. I was quite well acquainted with him after the

Emperor's visit. I followed the guy down a hall to a private room. There, the rather tall Ambassador in his rimless glasses was standing erect, with an aide on either side. I made the ritual bow, and he said: "Mr. Thorsell, the Guest House will be closing at 10 pm" It was about 9:30. I responded that, of course, there was a misunderstanding. We had booked the Guest House until 1 am (10:30, the "official" departure for Trudeau), and our guests were still arriving. "The Guest House will be closing at 10 pm," he repeated. I did the ritual bow and scurried back into the party to find Patrick Reid.

There are moments in our lives when you say to yourself, "I'm going to remember this."

***

I pulled Patrick away and shared the news. He told me to go back and request an immediate meeting between the two of them, both ambassadors. I ran back and found the Japanese Ambassador standing in exactly the same spot, with the same aides and the same mien. I communicated Ambassador Reid's request for an immediate meeting. He looked at his watch and said there was too little time before 10 pm, now just five minutes away.

I raced back to the party - now in full swing, lights, music, martinis, food, chatter – and informed Patrick. He took Trudeau aside to explain when a voice came over the loudspeaker saying the guest house would close in ten minutes. The lights dimmed, the bands lost their power, the food tables withdrew in a minute behind curtains, and Japanese staff began escorting our bewildered guests to the exit.

Reid and Trudeau were caucusing, and suddenly Trudeau jumped onto a chair and announced that the party would continue in the disco at the Quebec Pavilion, just beside the Canadian one. A cheer went up. The crowd poured out on their way across the site. A limousine was waiting for Trudeau with police escorts as we emerged from the guest house. I got in the back with him as Patrick and Alison headed off to the disco in a separate car.

We quickly came to a branch in the road where the driver was heading right for the freeway back to Osaka. I almost yelled, "to the left!" in Japanese. "We are staying on the Expo site!" He wavered, and I yelled again. He slowly turned to the left, the police escort regrouping in some disarray, and I instructed him on where to go. I didn't want the kidnapping of the prime minister of Canada to happen on my watch.

Two days later, Canadian Press photos showed Trudeau dancing in the disco at 2 am with a lovely young woman, capping off a brilliant Canadian National Day at Expo '70. Trudeau's scrapping of most of his formal agenda, including Ann of Green Gables, where the Japanese Ambassador was seated beside his chair, was a profound offence against protocol in a country that values protocol very highly indeed. The early closing of the Guest House was their revenge, I believed, and our relationship with them stayed cool for the duration. Happily, the Emperor had come and gone. And so had Trudeau.

***

Welcoming a Soviet Cosmonaut, at Expo 70

Some weeks earlier, I had received a letter from Princeton, obviously single-page within the thin envelope. Like most people, I have an aversion to rejection letters, so I didn't open it until I got home that evening, a cup of sake in my hand. The letter said I had been accepted in the Woodrow Wilson School of Public and International Affairs and, like the rest of my peers, tuition and room-and-board costs at the Graduate College were covered for the two years in attendance. In addition, each of us would receive a monthly stipend of $200 for expenses. Classes started in mid-September.

I had the new Beatles 'Abbey Road album in my apartment, with expressive Japanese script splayed across the front. I put it on, poured another sake, turned up the music and realized that my life was taking another decisive turn. Expo '70 ended in mid-September; I would have to leave Japan a bit early.

***

Most everyone had left the pavilion one muggy June evening when I got a call from the VIP entrance that we had an unannounced guest. They said it was Marlon Brando. Doubtful, I went down to find Marlon Brando standing there with a waif of a lovely Japanese woman. Could they tour the pavilion?

I brought them up to the VIP lounge, where my handsome Japanese waiter was still on-site and offered gin and tonic. We had one, then two, then three gazing out to the crowded courtyard below. Getting up after an hour or so to tour the pavilion, the young woman was clearly too woozy to make much headway. She laid down in a little sleeping room we had, and Marlon Brando and I headed downstairs for the tour. "Can we bring along another gin and tonic?" he asked. The waiter caught up with us a few minutes later with a tray and then again before we emerged from the tour near the stage in the courtyard.

A rock band was just about to perform at 8 pm for the crowd sitting in the seats around the stage. Brando was keen to hear it, so we ascended steep stairs to sit just under the control booth, high above it all. Our waiter appeared with another tray of gin.

"William – William," said Brando, asking how I had come by that name, rolling it around his mouth with those attractive lips. We talked about Japan and movies and Canada and Expo as the G&Ts kept flowing. An hour later, we somehow made it down the steep steps and back to the VIP suite, awoke his lady and emerged into the night. I walked them to the main gate, where their car was waiting, boarded the train for the one-stop to my apartment and called in sick the next day for the only time I worked at Expo '70.

Brando and I had a brotherly time, kibitzing and telling tales as though we were friends. Some 25 years later, my secretary told me that Marlon Brando was in Toronto making a movie and had contacted The Globe and Mail to say how much he admired our coverage of aboriginal affairs. He was willing to give an interview on the subject to our reporters. They went, he spoke, and we had a scoop that we shared that evening with The Wall Street Journal, as was our mutual agreement. I asked the reporter to remind Brando that he and I had met at the Canadian Pavilion in Japan in 1970, and he claimed no recollection of it.

We had a delicate crisis on Gabon's National Day, flying their flag alongside our own. Canada had recently restored diplomatic relations with French-speaking Gabon after Gabon had virtually recognized Quebec as an independent state some years before. Protocol dictated that Gabon's delegation visit Canada first among all other pavilions. Gabon decided, however, that they would visit the Quebec pavilion first and then come to Canada, which they did – an affront to protocol. After their visit to

Quebec, our commissioner-general met them at the outer edge of our pavilion, shook their hands and bid them farewell with no invitation to come inside. They departed, smirking.

Gabon was hosting a reception for all Commissioners General that evening, with Patrick Reid on the list, of course. In our morning meeting, Patrick confirmed there was no way he could attend, but he had a better idea than his simple absence as retaliation. "We'll send William in my place as a diplomatic insult!"

I was to arrive late and announce myself as Canada's representative, then leave immediately. It was raining. I made a conspicuous entrance wet, greeted the Gabon Head of Mission, and left on a heel. The whole management team was waiting in Patrick's office on my return to hear the gleeful tale, and a tray of gin and tonics was already sitting on the table. The Insult of William went well. We toasted my 25th birthday a few days later as the Irish Rovers sang on our pavilion stage.

***

John Diefenbaker heads to dinner

Former Prime Minister John Diefenbaker came for a couple of days. I went to the hotel in the pavilion car. He asked me up to his room. The door was ajar, and I found him reclining on his narrow bed, suited up and ready to go. Raising up, he rolled over onto the floor, which is how we met. I got him to his feet, and on we went.

Arriving in the lobby, Diefenbaker saw a red carpet leading to the front door, lined with officials of some sort. Instinctively, he headed down the carpet to be grabbed by a security officer and hauled to the side. Just then, the official delegation of Nigeria, splendid in their colourful robes, flowed out of the elevators and down the carpet, headed for their National Day. It was pouring rain, and I got the Chief to our modest car in the parking lot as quickly as possible.

I was hosting a dinner for 21 protocol officers at the Canadian pavilion that evening, while Mr. Diefenbaker was the guest of honour at the British pavilion with our commissioner-general. The phone rang, and it was my British counterpart saying Mr. Diefenbaker had left his hearing aid back at our pavilion, and the conversation was almost impossible. Mr. Diefenbaker had napped in our little guest room before leaving, and I said I would search for it and call back soon. A few minutes later, the British called again, saying they had found the device deep in Mr. Diefenbaker's ear. (I know something about these things these days.)

I returned to my guests, who enjoyed the story. We were serving Canadian wine from a jug discreetly wrapped in a cloth. "Tell me," asked the guy from Switzerland, "Is this wine made from grapes?"

On his departure from Osaka, Mr. Diefenbaker said I could ask him for one big favour sometime when I returned to Canada. A few years later, I did: It was to cooperate in a film documentary about his career, to which he readily agreed. We couldn't raise the money.

***

Completely involved by day, I felt increasingly alienated from protocol games and guilty about the many hierarchies and privileges that went with them. As the weeks passed, protocol started assuming the aura of the ridiculous to me, an affront to the spirit of the counter-culture times (of which I had just passing experience).

From an unsent letter written in Japan, March 1, 1970: "To date, working here has been ultimately shitty! Can you imagine! Protocol! I cannot imagine anything which is more the antithesis of the marvellous revolution of the '60s than my present occupation. It is torturing me. But of course, I am allowing it to torture me. I took this job, I accepted it. I am staying with it (although I would rather not – most emphatically!) Protocol – what a humiliation!"

I would have left early for Princeton in late August, but I pushed up the date to July 15 on this basis alone. Princeton gave me a pass, and I took it. Some months later, I wrote a letter to Patrick Reid explaining my discomfort and suggesting that such protocol functions be drastically reduced in future. Nothing came of that suggestion, of course: Protocol expressing hierarchy is human nature in all fields of endeavour.

Despite that, I loved and didn't love my time in Japan, more foreign to me than the USSR had been two years before. The culture was refined and civil, yet far too patterned for a guy from Alberta. ("Why can't they talk straight to the point!") The cities were dense and alive with variety, intimacy and people, the interior architecture sublime. I learned much about subtlety and grace in how the Japanese comported themselves. I learned how much better cuisine (and sake) could be. And I realized I was far too unkempt a Canadian to be Japanese.

Patrick Reid was a mentor in how confidently and strategically he made decisions and how he inspired trust among us all through example, participation and loyalty. We witnessed his standards and expectations and longed to meet them. I quietly referenced him many times in later careers, recalling his smarts and dignity in whatever context.

I brought back beautiful woodcut prints and a little wooden Shinto shrine presented to me with some ceremony by a Japanese family I had met. These talismans remain with me, and much more of the ineffable: I brought back some of the "observant" in Japanese culture, what might pass for "mindfulness" these days.

***

ON TO PRINCETON

On arrival at my parents 'house in Edmonton, I opened the garage door to my glistening, black 1966 Volvo coupe. Never has a black car been polished more carefully to look better in the shade.

A few weeks later, Gabino wrote from the Canadian Pavilion in Japan. He was originally an immigrant to the United States from Mexico and worked as a gardener in Oregon, but now was a dancer with the Feux Follets in Montreal, our resident dance company at Expo 70. Three weeks before I left Japan, Gabino was at dinner among my friends just down the hall from my apartment. As these things happened, it was late, and we decided he should stay with me overnight. And so I broke my vow on chastity for the moment.

Gabino was a beautiful man. Years of denial and abstinence rolled away on the futon and tatami mat that night. I never asked why he sought me out. And I was about to return to Canada.

About the same time, my handsome Japanese waiter approached one night working late to say he had missed his last train and had nowhere to stay: Could he come home with me? He, too, was beautiful and obviously potent. I had to say no – sleep on the couch here in the office – and went home. What would have happened if I had stayed through September in Osaka?

I was in Alberta in late July, and Gabino wrote to say he said he was returning to Canada early too (why?), and perhaps he could drop off in Edmonton on his way to Montreal. As these things happened, he stayed with me in Edmonton through August, and I dropped him off in Montreal on my drive across the continent to Princeton. Gabino was a gentle guy whom my mother adored. However, as I left Montreal for Princeton, I was convinced again that celibacy was essential and committed myself with more fervour to discipline as a condition of participation in a very interesting world. Lesson learned.

***

I had spent seven months of 1970 in Japan, working in luxurious circumstances with little access to news from abroad. Kent State was unknown to me.

I was out of the loop on cultural change and political events at home in these decisive years. I had no clear ideas on Vietnam nor many other issues of the time. I was not part of the sexual revolution – on the contrary. I was carried alongside the culture even as my closest friends became more passionately involved. I was born in 1945, one year ahead of the first baby boomer, and perhaps it mattered – just far enough ahead of the curve to miss it, so to speak.

At the same time, many of my cohorts also lived at a distance from the "popular culture." How many of us were actually like those rebellious kids on the news? Maybe I was more common in my sensibility than I knew. Maybe generational divides are less meaningful than we assume. Maybe generations are something of a passing show in a much more consistent picture.

***

I was 25 years old, arriving in Princeton with a pretty full CV. Most of my peers were 21 or so and had never been out of school. I didn't think about this at the time because I was coming from Alberta to – Princeton. But it would make a difference in how we all fared.

I drove into Princeton on a lovely afternoon and asked somebody how to find the Graduate College. She pointed to a gothic tower in the distance. As I drove down the road by the golf course, I thought, "They have made a terrible mistake in admitting me." I was enormously impressed and properly intimidated.

I had a pleasant, monkish room in the New Graduate College, recently built on more modernist and efficient lines alongside the Gothic original. There was a shared bathroom down the hall. We all mingled at breakfast in a cozy cafeteria. Dinner was held in the main chapel-like dining hall, sporting high, stained glass windows and an enormous pipe organ in the back. Dinner was at 6:30 sharp, served at long tables by undergraduates, each of us grad students required to wear a black robe over our street clothes. Used robes were on sale nearby, and I still have mine.

The introductory meeting of our cohort of 50 people at the Woodrow Wilson School was on Friday morning before classes started on Monday. We were ebullient, many of us having met already at the Grad College, where we had partied for several nights. A great weekend awaited.

Our welcome consisted of an assignment to read four short articles on zero-based budgeting (PPBS), compare and contrast them and submit our analysis on Monday morning in no more than four double-spaced, typed pages. Goodness. We were clearly at Princeton.

My first seminar on Monday was microeconomics, which would last two terms. The professor was a buxom young woman with exuberant red lips. This was 1970, when the counter-culture on campuses was still ascendant. She said something like this:

"Microeconomics is a foundation to understanding how the economy works and is quite complex. The reason I am standing up here, and you are sitting down there, is because I know a lot about microeconomics, and you know practically nothing. By the time you finish these semesters in April, you will know quite a lot – that is my commitment. For your part, you will miss none of our thrice-weekly classes, you will produce a weekly assignment, and you will pass the four major exams that will occur in these semesters. Yes: There is a power imbalance between us, and it is my goal to reduce it. If anyone here finds these conditions in some way unacceptable, please leave now."

There was a pause, and the room broke into applause. One person left.

A few weeks later, I was returning from the library with new friends around 11 pm, passing by the Princeton Theological Seminary under a big moon, and we stopped to talk about the fact we were at Princeton. David Buntain was from Nebraska, and we had found common ground in our thoughts. We made a pledge that being so lucky to be at Princeton, we would study hard indeed to merit the privilege. That is what we did.

Several days later, I was lying on my bed before dinner as sunlight slanted in, wondering how I possibly ended up in such a wonderful situation. What was the turning point? Who was the person who made the difference during a critical moment in a young man's trajectory?

I decided it was Hal Martin, the Alberta bureaucrat who had hired me to staff the Alberta booth at summer exhibitions in 1965 and 1966, and then who midwifed my appointment as Manager of the Western Canada Pavilion at Expo 67 when I was still just 20 years old. All these subsequent things had flowed from that.

I wrote him a letter that night expressing this view, addressed to "Hal Martin c/o The Government of Alberta, Edmonton, Canada: Trade and Industry Department," U.S. stamp on the envelope. Remarkably he received it. I still have his reply.

***

Our life was marvellous in the classroom and out. After dinner, we repaired to a TV room in the Graduate College to watch the CBS Evening News with Walter Cronkite, where we learned about the October crisis in Quebec (mentioned above). Then a group of us walked 30 minutes back to the library at WWS, staying until about 10:30. Sometimes, we stopped off at the Princeton University Chapel, where a music student gave a brief performance on the pipe organ every night at 11. Weekends offered forays onto Nassau Street to buy wine and dance parties at one of the colleges on site. (Viva Neil Young!) Sunday afternoon, we were back in the library. We took Princeton seriously even as we had some fun.

It soon became apparent that my somewhat older age and much wider experience set me aside a bit from my peers. Everybody asked initially about my Draft status: Had I been American, I had a very low number in the Draft lottery and would not have been called, but some classmates got the letter and tried various means to fail the medical (flat feet; starvation).

Being Canadian gave me some advantages over my American friends: I grew up in a small country looking out at the world, first at the U.S., but also as part of the Commonwealth and beyond. (My passport said, "A Canadian Citizen is a British Subject.") Observing the bigger world from a distance, you get to know it in ways that people at the centre do not – they live too close-up. Like growing up gay, a Canadian lived on a branch of the tree rather than in the trunk, so saw the whole thing from some distance and gained perspective.

Also, I had worked the fair circuit, did management in Montreal, camped through the Soviet Union, studied in Germany, written a grad thesis and lived in Japan. My very smart American fellow students were surprisingly parochial to me – because they were Americans and lived in a self-referenced world of their own. Most of them had always been in school. Not their fault.

We had "policy conferences" where my presentation skills rather stood out. And I had much more context to consider what I was reading and hearing in class. Several professors noted that I would remain silent through a three-hour seminar and then propose several big questions near the end that mattered. The value of "years out" through university is high, I realized. Schooling, like passion, delivers more value interrupted.

***

I had an offer to join the Privy Council Office in Ottawa for the summer of 1971 through Gordon Gibson, who was an aide to Trudeau when I was in Japan. There was another possibility in Beirut, with the Ford Foundation. Instead, I returned to Alberta to work for the Premier's office on cabinet reform and also for the Task Force on Urbanization and the Future in Alberta, headed by my friend Peter Boothroyd. I found a great little apartment on top of a house overlooking the river valley and settled in.

The project to reform Social Credit cabinet procedures fell apart immediately, as various ministers expressed astonishment and hostility that a grad student had any such mandate. (The cabinet barely offered agendas before meetings, and few of the ministers ' proposals for spending included anything like fiscal projections. Minutes were thin or even absent.) Thus, I spent the summer on the urbanization task force, meant to comprehend the implications that a shift from rural to urban populations in Alberta portended.

Meanwhile, Filmwest was powering ahead, and I had a great time with my friends, including Bob Reece, with whom I took weekend drives into the country. One Saturday, we went to Wetaskiwin, where I had started out as a baby in a garage. We found ourselves in a "junk store" where I noticed a jumble of wood parts that amounted to an old roll-top desk, like the one my maternal grandfather had. I bought it all for $120 – steep price then – and set it up as best I could in my little apartment, pieces barely holding together. I left it with other stuff in my parents 'basement when I returned to Princeton in September.

Bob and I spent many evenings that summer in Edmonton, often at my little apartment for dinner. I fell in love with him in the "wrong" way, and had to leave it be.

I returned at Christmas a few months later. My dad, Arne, picked me up at the airport and, when I walked into the house, I could smell something fresh and strange. We went to the basement where, under a golden light bulb, my roll-top desk gleamed with a sheen of teak oil, new canvas under the top, every surface sanded and re-stained, and every joint secure – a complete restoration by my father as a Christmas present. The roll-top is still the best design for a desk, with little drawers and cubbyholes to organize papers and display artifacts. Fifty years later, that desk remains a star asset in my Toronto apartment. My father loved me.

***

I worked for Social Credit Premier Harry Strom's government that summer, a progressive version of the 35-year-old regime that had existed under So-Cred's long-serving premier, Ernest Manning. The provincial election was slated for the end of August, and farmer Strom was up against Calgary's Peter Lougheed and the urban energy of the Progressive Conservative Party. Lougheed won a majority, and Tom Radford and I walked along Saskatchewan Drive, gazing across the valley to the Alberta Legislature. "This is the first time in my life I feel that Legislature belongs to me," I said. I was returning to Princeton within days but would show up again on Saskatchewan Drive.

***

The Graduate College held a lottery in the spring to determine choices for rooms in the coming year. I got a number near the top, and chose Room A in Pyne Tower, the top floor of the main building in the old Gothic Graduate College, up some 70 stone steps from the dining hall below. Classmates John Bayne and Charles Bailey chose Pyne Tower B and C, grouped around one shared bathroom. We effectively had the penthouse suite in the Old Grad College, with fireplaces, bookcases and seductive views over the golf course. We were set up for a fine year, playing Joni Mitchell's album Blue along with Led Zepplin. (After Montreal, this was my second penthouse with friends – and not the last.)

Somewhere during these months, a group of us composed a letter to the faculty suggesting how we thought the Woodrow Wilson School could improve its curriculum. It led to a meeting with professors, and I recall an open-minded discussion that would have consequences for me a few years later.

***

The year went wonderfully as we came into the spring of 1972. I had taken a course in the Faculty of Architecture and Urban Planning, and decided to study in their library one evening for access to books. As usual, an undergraduate was earning tuition by staffing the desk. He was an attractive black guy, and we kept meeting eyes as I studied at my table. On leaving the next night, we got talking and agreed to meet the night after for a coffee after closing.

He took me to his room, painted black and decorated in colourful textiles. It had been almost two years since

Gabino, and I was thrilled with our physical encounter – and scared. He was intriguing, studying architecture on his way, he hoped, to Harvard. I stayed away from his library after that but ran into him at the post office a few weeks later. He said he was worried by my absence, and there was nothing to fear. (But I did fear.) I never saw him again, but the dam was breaking.

(In 2017, I got an email from him through the Princeton alumni network. He did go to Harvard, had a successful career, and was now living back near Princeton.)

***

Our final exams at Woodrow Wilson lasted a week, including three-hour written tests, on economic policy in my case and, finally, an oral exam before four professors. Then it was off to a bar in a nearby village where we saw on TV that someone had just shot Alabama Governor George Wallace.

Bob Reece was arriving from Alberta, and we were heading for a few weeks to Europe to meet up with his girlfriend, so I would miss my graduation. The day I moved out of the Graduate College was surprisingly tough. We all met by Cleveland Tower, where my Volvo was ready to go. I was deeply saddened to realize that our little community was probably gone forever. There was no Internet – no Facebook; letters would soon tire us out. We would go our separate ways.

I had job possibilities in Washington, New York, Chicago and Ottawa on graduation. Instead, I decided to return to Edmonton and Filmwest Associates to make documentaries. My friends were doing well; I had things to offer.

Besides, I had made a promise with a Mexican friend at WWS that we would each return to our countries to use the Princeton education at home rather than stay in the United States. Twenty-five years later, as editor-in-chief of The Globe and Mail, I visited Manuel Camacho at his office, where he was Mayor of Mexico City and a possible successor to President Carlos Salinas (also a WWS graduate). Manuel eventually ran for President of Mexico as an independent, then dropped out after the assassination of the PRI candidate that year. He died too young of cancer.

Bob and I returned from Europe a few weeks later and picked up my car in Princeton, where I had parked it with another WWS friend, Chuck Krause. Many years later, Chuck was the reporter who survived the Jonestown massacre in Guiana, hiding behind the wheel of a small airplane on a grassy runway, and he wrote a compelling book about it. We had lunch in Toronto some years later and marvelled at our journalistic histories in retrospect.

Bob and I drove west, arriving in Medicine Hat late at night. The next morning, we decided to go back-country to Edmonton, on gravel roads through Drumheller and up past Camrose. It was a hot day in May, and we stopped the car in a golden prairie expanse with no sight of a power pole. We could hear only meadowlarks. "I will find this loveliness again," I said to myself. But not the core of it: I was saying goodbye to my own private Bob as we returned to life in Edmonton. Gay, I was alone, I knew.

send me a

flower

black-petalled

yet

a flower

just

the same

ask me a

question

no answers

possible;

yet

ask of me

again

bring me your

body

immaculate

love

unyielding still?

then

forget me

your

name

May 1972

What was I thinking? Why was it clear to me, after all my adventures, that I would not take one of those hot jobs after Princeton and instead return to Alberta and Filmwest, where I had no real history? I had no income. Filmwest was a small operation that had grown entirely in my absence. What was I expecting? I had made an enormous investment (as had Princeton) in my education, had diverse work experience, and here I was returning to Edmonton to work with my friends without a plan.

I have no explanation for that. I wanted to go home.

***

SENATE, U OF A: GAY AT LAST

It soon became apparent that film was not my medium in any case. Film works slowly in creating stories and, for documentaries in those days, reached few people. I soon realized that my personal narrative had to pick up again in some other realm. So what to do?

I read an advertisement in the Edmonton Journal, sitting on my mother's front porch in August 1972. It sought the first Executive Officer of the Senate at the

University of Alberta, half-time. I applied to the Chancellor, Louis Desrochers was interviewed and hired. I had a familiar base again – and better – it was a start-up. (I wonder what would have happened had I not seen that ad that day.)

The Senate was some 50 people meant to bring together the university's various constituencies, including importantly the public. It was composed of faculty, students and "public representatives," chaired by the Chancellor and having few actual powers – it was a consultative body – except for choosing recipients of honorary degrees. (I kept nominating Joni Mitchell, but no one on the committee knew who she was.) The Senate had never had any real staff. Louis Desrochers, a youngish francophone lawyer and newly Chancellor of the University, chaired the Senate. He wanted to bring its mandate to life just, as it happened, I returned to Alberta.

Within a few months, we created a strategy for the Senate that focused on Task Forces into issues of shared university-community interest (tenure, the future of neighbourhoods bordering the university, campus planning, student finance). And soon, my position was full-time. With Louis in the chair, the Senate became influential, holding some quarterly meetings in places such as Red Deer and Camrose. It was a stimulating, constructive experience, where I met many interesting people, including Chester Ronning and Stevie Munro, wife of the publisher of the Edmonton Journal, Ross Munro.

Louis Desrochers was a leading Liberal party supporter in Alberta and had me appointed to a jury of the Canada Council – the federal arts granting agency. I was soon chairman of the prairie and northern Canada jury for the "Explorations Program," which supported emerging artists in any field – textiles, painting, music, sculpture. We considered applications three times a year, and I then went to Ottawa to hash out the national grants among my regional colleagues. Our most memorable meeting was in Providence, NWT, after travelling for a week on a Twin Otter from Yellowknife to Coppermine to Goa Haven and Spence Bay, visiting artist coops. We had funded five women in Spence Bay to die wool from coloured tundra plants and to weave tapestries on felt usually meant for parkas. I bought one of them, as well as an abstracted head in stone from an ancient man in Goa Haven. We discovered myriad creative impulses in "ordinary people" over the five years I served – another gift of a great assignment.

A year into this, I received a letter from the Woodrow Wilson School in Princeton, asking if I would be interested in returning as Director of Admissions for the graduate program. I had started a new life in Edmonton and declined.

***

Anne Wheeler and I had met as undergraduates at U of A, at fraternity exchange parties where we learned we were both pretty good on the piano and something of performers as well. Our paths crossed again during the summer of 1970, when she returned from a long trip in Africa and got seriously involved with Filmwest. As I started my job at the university Senate in 1972, we agreed to rent a house together beside the campus as buddies.

Anne Wheeler and I, 1974

Two months earlier, sitting around with my friends at Cheryl Malmo's house, the conversation got into relationships and, seemingly out of nowhere, I told everybody that I was gay. It was liberating not just for me, but for them, who were trying to understand my sometimes oblique behaviours. No one was really surprised, though I was amazed (the dam broke at 27). So Anne and I shared the house as buddies. That is when she planted the seeds for her film, "War Story," based on the diaries of her father, a doctor who had been interned in a Japanese prisoner of war camp on Taiwan throughout the Second World War. Anne was budding into a major feature film-maker.

***

We visited auctions, and I bought a lovely upright piano that had come from Argentina, and sounded quite good. I bought an oak sideboard and refinished it in the basement. Anne bought some beautiful chairs and a dining table, having brought along a pedal organ and a big couch from her family's collection. We set up a rather fine home.

One year later, we rented a more commodious house down the block, and another friend moved in to share space and expenses – Gail Price. We were all single in the late '20s and looking for action. We'd often go our separate ways on Saturday nights. Sunday morning, I would come down the stairs and count the boots by the front door. "Oh, three extra guys for breakfast this morning, who have never met each other or two of us." I would put more eggs and pancakes on the stove.

***

I was offered a column in the university's monthly alumni magazine, New Trail, to write about anything. One of those columns was titled "The Trials of the Golden-Haired Boy" (August 1974). Aware by now of how important it was to my sensibility that I was gay, and remembering my mother's fear that I would settle down to a predicted life in Edmonton, I pondered the price that comes with being part of the dominant baby boom generation. I didn't announce myself as gay in this largely autobiographical article, but it was the subtext. Here is an excerpt:

"Living within bulge [baby boomer] society is so pervasive an experience, and often so untroubled, that our personal intellectual and artistic growth may be stunted. We may never have the kind of alienating experiences that generate higher levels of consciousness. If, in addition to being part of the baby boom, one also happens to be a white, blue-eyed, blond, protestant male, the likelihood of experiencing truly human growth may be even less likely. With all of our apparent advantages, we may be labelled as an ugly generation – like the North American tourist, securely prosperous and self-confident but, almost as a consequence, sadly limited in his orientation to other realities.

"The value in being part of a bulge must be seriously questioned. In fact, minorities may be the lucky ones.... In contrast to those in the majority, minority people become aware at an early age of at least two realities – their own and that of all those who are so obviously different. They, therefore, tend to gain a more complex understanding of the world simply as a function of their minority position.... Minority people's thoughts are more likely to turn to philosophy and politics, their hands to painting or music than those of the superficially fortunate golden-haired boy.... Because minority people are not, in some sense, part of the bulge, they are more likely to live awake."

I'm not sure that being gay qualified me as a real minority by then, given my conspicuous luck and privileges, but I do think I foresaw the consequences of ageing boomers rather well:

"When we reach our sixties, if we wish to remain employed, we will successfully eliminate artificial retirement requirements. We will energetically attack all ageist attitudes and claim 'natural 'prior rights over the young. As we have to date, we will assume that society exists for us, that we are a group meriting emulation, that we are the people in control. In time, we will reorient society to old age as surely as we presently orient society to youth…. Simply because we are the bulge, we will carry social reality with us, and each of us will therefore inherit a somewhat easier life."

***

Anne and I had little pocket money then, and would save up to buy two drinks each at a lounge downtown on Wednesday nights. We would sit separately, me at the piano bar, trolling for love. Most times, we would go home together, but sometimes I would go home alone. Then one night, I met a guy there, and Anne went home alone. It was fall, 1973. He was my first gay contact in Edmonton, and opened another world to me.

He came to dinner at our house one Friday night and suggested we two leave about 10 pm for a gay bar downtown. I had never been to one and resisted, but we went. The crowded parking lot surrounded a one-story cinder-block building in a deserted industrial area. We entered a vestibule where a guy behind a glass booth checked my friend's membership card, then buzzed us into the bar. Suddenly, behind a thick metal door, we entered a throbbing disco, lights, music, booze, men and women. It was Club '70, Edmonton's first gay and lesbian bar, open only Friday and Saturday nights. I rarely missed another weekend there, thrilled at the brotherly outlaw status it gave, not to mention access to guys. I soon broke up with my handsome lounge lizard and moved on.

(He had been through conversion therapy as a student at the University of Alberta. They attached electrodes to his body and asked him to turn pages in a magazine that showed either sexy women or sexy men. He got an electric shock each time a sexy male appeared. "Well," I said, sitting next to him in bed, "that obviously didn't work." On the contrary: He could no longer flip through magazines.)

***

In the pit at Walterdale

One bitter winter night, Anne and I heard a loud cracking sound from the dining room. Our Argentinian piano was splitting apart in the extremely dry air, and now became unplayable.

I needed a piano, and checked the ads for something used. Incredibly, a Steinway Grand was for sale at a very low price. In the foyer of a mansion downtown, it sat – old and unplayable. But oh – don't you know this was the Yamaha piano dealership in Edmonton, 1973! And the rest of the rooms were filled with brand new Yamahas, the grievous Steinway acting as the lure.

I traded in my Argentinian piano on a new Yamaha G2 grand, deciding on the spot that I would put off the new car I really wanted. They would deliver it on a November Friday evening.

I didn't tell Anne, and we had friends for dinner that night. The doorbell rang about 8 pm, and I opened it to the sight of a large truck backed up to the front porch as cold-fogged air flooded into the house. Within an hour, we had a new grand piano set up in the living room, and I still possess it. Singing ensued.

By then, I was acting in plays at the Walterdale Theatre, an accomplished amateur community group, and began composing music for its annual summer melodrama, which played at the Citadel Theatre downtown during "Klondike Days," Edmonton's forlorn answer to the Calgary Stampede. I played a big old upright piano below the stage through the play and created four or five original songs for the leads and chorus to sing. (I aimed my best songs at Wheeler.) This relationship with Walterdale continued into the late 1970s. I still have many of the songs.

Here is the text of my first song written for theatre, 1973:

I was around when Jesus Christ was young and
handsome,

I was in view when Mary had her child,

But I've never seen a situation quite like this one:

The universe is going wild.

People will tell you always put your faith in logic,

People will say beware the ways of love,

But I'm one of those who gets a little bit nostalgic

Just give my heart a gentle shove.

[Music on the radio, blue moon shining in the sky

Who knows how far to go

Should you go all the way, oh baby yi, yi, yi]

Everything good in life will come to those who'll wake it

Happiness is to which you can aspire

Good fortune isn't something that you get – you make it

So set your lazy hearts on fire!

***

I was examining a cuckoo-clock work of art in the
Douglas Udell gallery downtown one Saturday afternoon
and felt a presence beside me. He turned out to be a
University of Alberta lecturer and grad student from a

174

francophone town in Alberta. We exchanged numbers, and Gerard became my first full-fledged boyfriend.

Gerard had gone to a French-speaking Catholic boarding school in his local town starting in Grade 7. As the boys went to bed in the dormitory at 9 pm, a priest would describe the scene in an opera, or movement in a symphony they would be hearing as the lights went out. Gerard was an encyclopedia of music and the literary classics in a way no public school guy from Edmonton could ever be. Our vibrant relationship continued for some three years, keeping separate houses but entwining in the most wonderful ways. He described himself as a "sex machine," and there was ample truth in that. But his brain was his most erotic organ and his culture his greatest gift.

***

In the spring of 1974, the phone rang at my University of Alberta Senate office. It was someone I did not know, Donald Stokes, Dean of Graduate Studies at the University of Michigan in Ann Arbor. He said he would be the new Dean of the Woodrow Wilson School of Public and International Affairs at Princeton, starting that July. He wanted to do a thorough review of the undergrad and graduate curricula at WSS, right off the top. Would I be interested in coming back to Princeton to work with him on this as "Special Assistant to the Dean?"

I flew down to Ann Arbor for a weekend with Don and his wife Sybil, staying at their wonderfully modernist house in the woods. Don and I went for several long walks in the fields discussing the WWS. Some faculty there had remembered our student papers suggesting improvements a few years earlier, which is why he had called me.

I thought it a wonderful project and suggested that we put off my arrival for a year so he could get a read on the faculty and politics of the situation. I knew enough about WWS to realize there were many conflicting interests, and this would be a delicate and challenging task. To my mind, the school had been somewhat "colonized" by existing university departments: We needed a declaration of independence as a unique school of public policy. I thought Stokes would do well to observe things alone at the outset – then we could make plans when I came a year later. He responded that the best time for initiatives like this was at the outset when the new Dean had fresh authority, scope and benefit of the doubt.

We got along very well, and I said I would ponder it and get back soon.

I was discussing this with Anne Wheeler and friends at Giuseppi's pizza parlour back in Edmonton, expressing my skepticism about the timing of all this, when Anne posed a very straight question: "What is really holding you back from making this move?" In the course of my reply, I said I was happy and very comfortable being back in Edmonton among my friends. "Comfortable!" exclaimed Anne. "You're still not 30, and you are turning down great opportunities because you're 'comfortable'?"

It wasn't the only reason, but it was clearly one, and I couldn't abide it. I had Don Stokes 'home number in my wallet, went over to the pay phone in the restaurant and called him to say I was keen to come and get to work. "You start September 1," he said. I would return to Princeton two years after graduation on a most intriguing assignment.

***

Anne Wheeler's focus on that word "comfort" was something of a life lesson and recalled my mother's concern that I was too much a homebody, and might end up as a decent executive living in an Edmonton suburb. "You're not going to hang around here, are you?" was one of her two quiet admonitions. (The other was, "You're not feeling sorry for yourself, are you?" – to Irene, self-pity was dreadful and, in my case, inconceivable.)

In later years, when waffling about some new commitment, I would hear Anne's awful word "comfort" and push ahead. I appreciate comfort as a state but oppose it as an operating principle.

Ultimately, I recast this awareness with my own adage: "No is a much bigger word than Yes" when facing a close choice. What does this mean? Through experience, I realized, not only does *Yes* expose you to new worlds but *Yes* is generally reversible if it doesn't work out. *No*, in contrast, is generally irreversible – if your original "No" was a mistake, you cannot generally go back and offer *Yes* later: The "yes" was taken.

 No: Irreversible. Yes: Reversible.

You can say Yes to marriage and get divorced. You can buy and property and sell it. You can move away – and move back. You can take a job and quit it.

You can say *No* to a smart young man whom you love and never get him back when you realize your mistake.

In sum, the risk/reward of *Yes* is much more attractive than that of *No* in close calls. I said *Yes* to Princeton, and used this *Yes/No* adage many times in my management careers years later.

By the way, I also believe in the excellent power of *No*, when you know just why.

***

PRINCETON AGAIN

Gerard rode down to Princeton with me that August in my burnt-orange 1972 Alfa Romeo coupe, which I saw in a used-car lot in Edmonton, tried out and bought on the spot in 1974. Gerard flew back west a few weeks later from New York. I had an endearing one-bedroom apartment provided by Princeton on the main floor of a clapboard house on Alexander Street, just beside campus. I had a spiffy faculty office on the top floor of the Woodrow Wilson School. And I had a letter from WWS professor Michael Danielson, welcoming me back, saying the assignment was going to be difficult indeed:

"Having said the nice words, let me say that you have let yourself in for an arduous task – my biggest and perhaps the saddest lesson from the past few years is how difficult it is to secure changes in a complex, successful and decentralized bit of academe like the Woodrow Wilson School. Not impossible to be sure, and certainly worth trying, but very tough. We have so many diverse constituencies, our personnel resources are stretched to the limit, and we are pushing the limits of our income. All of which means that change affects fundamental interests – and increasingly means that change is redistributive rather than additive as it has been during the past decade or so."

This I understood, which is why I had advised the new Dean to observe the landscape for a year before my arrival.

Don and Sybil Stokes were wonderful people, and I often went to their home for dinner. Don had a marvellous corner office overlooking the campus, and each Friday at 5 pm, three or four of us would gather there as he made martinis from an elegant sideboard, something like we had at Expo '70. After martinis, I would wander 30 minutes through campus to my house on the other side, struck by the beauty and delight of it all. I envied the students of whom I was no longer one.

We prepared a working document and met the faculty in late October, where Don described his goals and our approach to the curriculum review. A few hands went up with careful and opaque questions about the need or urgency for all this. The gentle skepticism gained steam, and then one of the most senior faculty rose and made a motion that this worthy project return for consideration in the following academic year. It passed quickly with almost unanimous consent. Michael Danielson patted me on the back in consolation on the way out.

It was only a Tuesday night, but Don and I repaired to his office for martinis. I would have to find something else to do.

***

Back in the library of the WWS, I immediately noticed a change in the flavour of the student body just two years after my graduation. The guys were preppy-dressed, with V-neck sweaters and slacks, the women in nice blouses and pleated skirts. In contrast, my cohort had arrived out of the late '60s and looked like it, jeans, rough shirts and all. By 1974, the new class at Woodrow Wilson was of another generation, both younger and older, maybe kids of the "silent majority."

We all read The New York Times. One day, I saw something about Canada I thought was misleading. I wrote them a letter. A couple of days later, walking through campus, several people said, "Saw your letter in the Times!" There it was, and everybody had seen it.

The Times published my second letter some weeks later, and I realized how powerful was the reach of the newspaper – powerful and immediate. You could reach a million people overnight, and the next night too. For a guy working in a school of public policy, the newspaper appeared to be far superior a medium to academic

182

papers or, indeed, documentary film. Here was a route to really using my education and experience effectively before a broad audience daily.

Meanwhile, Don Stokes tried to come up with things for me to do – a little research into this or that, some information-gathering about other universities' programs. But there was nothing much to do, and I whiled away the days in growing boredom. Early in December, I gave him a memo asking for new terms of reference that would make for real work. His reply was kind and evasive. By the time I headed back to Edmonton for Christmas, I knew I wanted something more.

***

During Christmas week, I borrowed my dad's car and drove around town. I went past the little house I had rented the previous summer and followed the road through some woods to Skunk Hollow, two short streets tucked under Saskatchewan Drive along the riverbank across from downtown. Here was a small house for sale backing on the North Saskatchewan River itself, with great views of the valley and city.

There was an open house on January 30. I went with my father, who pronounced the foundation sound and, as other people wandered around, I wrote up an offer on the kitchen table. They were asking $35,000. My dad said I should offer no more than $30,000. People kept milling around, and I wrote down $32,000. I said, "I'm not going to lose this house for $2,000," and besides, I was returning to Princeton the next day.

My dad called the following week to say the house was mine. (I should have offered the full asking price, so wonderful was that property. I sold it six years later for $123,000.)

On many occasions, I recalled that sentiment: "I'm not going to lose this house for $2,000." When you really want something important, you don't risk it for small change – which I have witnessed in others many times. I applied this lesson to my own choices in later years to good effect.

This idea evolved into another one of my adages: "Some people believe that if you count the pennies, the dollars will take care of themselves. In contrast, I believe that if you count the dollars, the pennies will take care of themselves." Focus on the big picture, get it right, and be not a prisoner of the details – though some details deserve more attention, perhaps, than I am wont to give them. "Count the dollars, and the pennies will take care of themselves." Then peace be upon you.

Don Stokes called me in Edmonton over Christmas, and I confirmed that I would be leaving WWS at the end of January. He remonstrated, I stuck firm, and he said he was sure I would return, and he would keep that position open indefinitely. I never stopped liking that man, who succumbed to a brain tumour much too young some years later.

Throughout the fall at Princeton, I drove on weekends 45 minutes to New Hope, Pennsylvania in Buck's County, on the Delaware River, famous for its gay bars. It was a hilly, curvy road in my Alfa Romeo coupe, radio booming, which ended with a dramatic arrival over the river on a big steel bridge. The major bars were the Cartwheel and the New Prelude, packed each weekend with great guys in the age of disco. We danced and danced, and most times, I found myself in someone's suburban apartment overnight or led them back to Princeton at 1 am. My last weekend there in January, I clicked with a guy I had been watching for weeks at the New Prelude, and we had a vigorous night together at his place nearby on the river. He was a carpenter and so much more, but it was my last weekend in town. We kept in touch, then lost it.

On weekend trips to New York, only an hour away by train, I sought out gay life too. I met a guy at an Italian bar downtown one afternoon, went home with him and didn't realize until then that he had lost one arm to an accident in youth. (I was distracted by other virtues.) I met another beautiful black guy at a bar on Third Avenue who, like me, had acted in The Mikado in school, and we belted these songs out wandering along 42nd Street to my hotel at 1 am Brotherhood was often fleeting but brotherhood nevertheless.

**

PART TWO: NEWSPAPERS

THE EDMONTON JOURNAL

I had met Stevie Munro at the University of Alberta Senate, where she was a lively public member. I socialized a bit with her and her husband, the famous war correspondent Ross Munro, who was now publisher of the Edmonton Journal. An appetite whetted by my letters published in the New York Times, I asked Ross if there might be a position at the Journal as a commentator/analyst. I was not after a job as a reporter. He replied that, indeed, he had two positions opening on the editorial board in the summer of 1975, and I could join on a three-month trial basis. I was elated.

Meanwhile, Chancellor Louis Desrochers came to my aid with a short-term contract for the Glenbow Museum in Calgary, where he was on the board. I spent the spring touring regional museums in Alberta to see how Glenbow's outreach programs could be improved. It took me to fascinating little places in my conspicuous Alfa Romeo. My report concluded that regional museums actually wanted more profile at the Glenbow itself, in addition to certain other aids. Thirty years later, I would create just such a program for regional Ontario museums in Toronto as CEO of the Royal Ontario Museum.

Ross Munro sent me a note of welcome to the Edmonton Journal in August 1975, saying he had never regretted a moment of his life in newspapers, and hoped I wouldn't either. And I didn't, except for the day I walked out the door at The Globe and Mail, 25 years later.

Diary entry, January 10, 1968: "I cannot be satisfied with the attainment of personal happiness characterized by wife, home, 'job 'and social acceptance. For my 'metier 'must be more than 'job, 'it must be the central justification for my life. As such, it must involve, profoundly – man and creativity and expansion. My context has to become three billion [people]; thus, my task in ideals must assume equal scope."

***

My father, Arne, came to my little two-story house every evening to help renovate. (I put $5,000 down and had a $27,000 mortgage.) I dug up the front lawn to plant vegetables. We removed a wall between the living room and a bedroom, creating a beautiful space that could accommodate my Yamaha grand and that lovely roll-top desk. We removed a wall between the kitchen and back porch, creating a dining room in the latter, with great views of the river and city, just in time for Arne's 60th birthday on April 1 (yes, Fool's Day). I did steaks and vodka, of course, and we realized that 1975 would be the only year when he would be exactly twice my age – me turning 30 in July. And when Arne was 990 years old, and I was 960, we would be indistinguishable. In fact, it happens much more quickly. When he died at 86, I was quickly morphing into my dad at 56.

The speed that time passes concerns the denominator: Two months of a summer holiday when you are eight years old is a much bigger fraction of your life than two months when you are 60. That earlier summer goes on forever; the latter reminds you that forever is approaching quickly.

Arne noticed that a double-hung window in the living room was off-centre, crooked. He suggested we take it out, remake the frame and put it back in straight-up. I demurred. To Arne, the window was a fault that needed fixing. I argued it was an eccentricity that gave character to the place, authenticity and made the house even more beautiful as a consequence. Blemishes that arise over time can enhance the boring perfection of the original – patina, we call it. Arne came around to that view, and we enjoyed that errant window evermore. (An ageing flower bouquet dropping petals on a table makes as beautiful a tableau as the fresh thing.)

Occasionally, Arne turned up to help on a Sunday morning when there was a nubile guy sitting with me at breakfast after the club night before. I would make introductions, more eggs, and we'd carry on, not explicit but aware.

***

I wrote editorials for the Edmonton Journal, and one day, the editor, Andy Snaddon, suggested I write a signed column on something I had vented about that morning. And so my first signed column in late August 1975 argued that Premier Peter Lougheed should reject calls to enter the federal Progressive Conservative leadership race that fall because he was far too important to Alberta only four years after his election to leave Alberta in the lurch. He would betray the province and the "New West." Two days later, Andy Snaddon told me that Lougheed had called and asked who that Thorsell kid was.

Lougheed stayed out of the contest, Joe Clark won, and the drama continued. Peter Lougheed and I became well acquainted over time. When I suggested in print that he had quit the 1983 federal Tory leadership race because he would lose, he sent me a hand-written note saying he would have won. Lougheed had entered the race primarily to block Ontario Premier Bill Davis and, when Davis quit, so went Lougheed. We would meet for lunch in Toronto after he retired, Lougheed always hinting that I had let Alberta down myself by leaving town.

***

In May 1976, I decided to take a week's holiday in Toronto, where I had last worked at the CNE in 1966. Toronto was Canada's leading English-speaking city, and I wanted to check it out again, not to mention the gay scene.

I found the St. Charles gay pub on my first night there, met a good guy two days later at another pub and became infatuated with him, the city and the future. I returned to Edmonton determined to leave.

I gathered together a few more signed columns and sent copies to the editors of the three Toronto "celestial" papers - Star, Globe and Sun – asking for work on their editorial boards. Within a week, I got a letter from the Sun saying it was not a good fit. Weeks later, I got a letter from the Star expressing interest and saying they would pay for me to visit them in August, to which I readily agreed. Nothing came from The Globe.

I was working in my garden one evening in July where I heard the phone ringing inside. It was Dic Doyle, editor-in-chief of The Globe and Mail, saying he had just got around to reading his mail and was interested in seeing me. I told him I was already booked to see the Star on a Monday in mid-August. Too bad, he replied, he would be at his cottage that week. Could I come a few days earlier and see him the previous Friday. Agreed.

I wore my best baby-blue gabardine suit with wide lapels and a flowered tie to complement my full moustache and unruly hair. I spent 90 minutes with Dic in his office in the early afternoon discussing many things, including Ronald Reagan's prospects at the Republican convention that month: He wouldn't win against Gerald Ford, I intoned. We got up to leave, and, as we got to the door, he asked, "When can you start?"

"Start what?" I replied. "Work on the editorial board," he said quite simply. I blurted out in late September. Agreed. He took me to meet the Managing Editor, Grant Davey, who would look after my moving expenses. Then I walked into a hot August afternoon on Front Street West, looking for a phone booth.

I called David Crane at the Toronto Star and said I would not be coming in on Monday as I had just been hired by The Globe. As I walked downtown, I realized my life was going to change meaningfully again and then wondered what my salary would be at The Globe. We hadn't discussed it.

***

Three weeks before my trip to Toronto, I dropped into Flashback, a new gay bar in Edmonton, on my way home from dinner with friends. It was about 11 pm, and I saw a very handsome guy standing alone near the dance floor, nursing a beer. I slipped up next to him, so if he moved at all, he would bump into me. And he did.

Monty and I ended up living together for six years, through the tumult and good times both. He was 25 to my 31 in 1976, and had just graduated with a bachelor's degree in fine arts from the University of Alberta. He was a painter. He was recently married.

I told Monty that I was hoping to move to Toronto soon. We had no past, and I imagined no future either. As it happened, we spent each night together, and he came with me to Toronto two months later and enriched my life – perhaps helped save it for the third time.

We were watching the news one Sunday night in 1981, which described a dangerous new disease affecting gay men in the United States. I immediately said, "It's from the baths," where gay men enjoyed great promiscuity at will. No one knew what this affliction was exactly, but we saw off the top that it was an STD.

I often think that if I had not met Monty on that July evening in 1976 and gone on to Toronto as a single man in subsequent years, I would not be alive today. We unwittingly took ourselves out of circulation just when it was critical to do so.

***

Off to Toronto, 1976 - Photo Credit, Richard Gishler

I was thrilled to join the Editorial Board at The Globe in September 1976. We met each day at 11 am, with Dic Doyle in the chair, his trusty 2-IC Jean Howarth to his right, four more of us perched around. In Edmonton, our board meeting started with a take from each person on what was happening and what we should be saying about it. We'd talk it out, agree on assignments and be done in an hour.

Dic's board room was dark and woody, and he among several people smoked – the room became a smoke-box.

He started off with a monologue, often 45 minutes or so, on whatever – Judy Garland in a certain film, the quality of new public housing developments in Toronto. Then at some point, he would look to one of us and say, "On page A17, there is a story about child neglect in Niagara," and whoever got that nod started writing notes as Dic expressed his views.

I soon learned that it was our job to wait for the look from Dic, take notes, then do some research and try to put his views into paragraphs through the afternoon. We delivered our copy to his office by 5:30. It would come back amended with scribbles in the margins. We then sent it to the composing room in plastic tubes through a vacuum system, and it appeared the next day as a Globe and Mail editorial. (One of us checked the final page proof in the composing room, still using hot lead type in the emerging computer age: smoke in the board room, lead in the composing room.)

I found this alienating and even rather pathetic. Sometimes, one of us got more rope, but not often. At the end of January, I went to Jean Howarth to ask how I was doing and to say that I would embrace any suggestions Dic might have about my work. She said I wouldn't be there if he was unhappy with me, and that was that.

The phone rang in February. It was J. Patrick O'Callaghan, who had arrived as Publisher of the Edmonton Journal some months before my departure. He asked how I was doing, and I said it was "different." He made a strong case that I was in the wrong place at the wrong time – I should be back in the burgeoning West, in charge of the editorial pages at the Journal, the voice of the New West in Canada, associate editor of the Edmonton Journal, a star! Besides, I would be in management, have a significantly better salary – and a car!

Dic was on holiday when I informed Jean Howarth that I would be leaving at the end of March. Dic said nothing on his return and, on my last day at The Globe, after I filed my piece, his secretary brought me a note from him on yellow foolscap saying thanks and good luck. Jean told me that no one who quit The Globe was ever hired back.

***

Monty had left his wife and joined me in Toronto that December. We were soon battling, and he decided to stay in Toronto, living in the painting studio we rented for him in an old industrial building on The Esplanade (now the home of Diamond-Schmidt Architects). So I drove north onto the trans-Canada highway on a lovely morning in late March, headed for Edmonton and a new/old life. Rather than sell, I had wisely rented out my house in Skunk Hollow and would soon get it back.

North of Lake Superior, my Alfa Romeo started making noise and losing power in an enormous snowstorm. I got the last room in a motel somewhere in the dark.

***

I had returned to Edmonton several times already, from Montreal in 1967, from Princeton in 1972 and 1975, and now, in 1977, from Toronto after only six months away. I had some kind of romantic or psychological attachment to Alberta that brought me back. This time would cure me of that and instil a deep aversion to "going back" in almost every circumstance.

Edmonton's skyline came into view on the Yellowhead Highway and looked distinctly drab after Toronto. April is the cruellest month in Edmonton, especially, all brown and dusty, the winter's street sand piled up at intersections waiting to be trucked away, blowing in the wind. I returned to the Journal downtown and was soon overwhelmed with regret that I had left Toronto, despite the pleasures of my new job. And I missed Monty despite our travails.

After some back-and-forth, Monty returned in December, and we created a household in Skunk Hollow. It was something of a life-saver.

***

Peter Lougheed was Premier of Alberta, and J. Patrick O'Callaghan was publisher of the Edmonton Journal. I commanded the editorial pages, from editorials to letters to op-eds – three full pages every day. I ranged broadly in sources, frequently wrote under my own name, and soon became something of a fixture in the Alberta scene.

J. P. O'C, as we called him, had a direct relationship with Lougheed and every few months arranged lunch at the Edmonton Club or nearby hotel with the Premier and myself. We started with martinis, then excellent wines. Over time, Lougheed came to trust our discretion and confide in us more.

In 1979, Lougheed won all 79 seats in the Legislature, and J. P. O'C declared in a front-page editorial (which none of us had seen) that the Journal would now serve as the Unofficial Opposition to the government. Actually, though, we were firmly on Lougheed's side in the coming wars over energy and the Constitution with Pierre Trudeau's resurrected regime. (Lougheed told me the real opposition existed within his caucus – terribly parochial people from rural constituencies. He said he would have much preferred they had their own party and sat, visible, across the aisle as Official opposition, where he could ignore them. Perhaps that has not changed in Alberta.)

We lunched with Lougheed during Joe Clark's brief term as prime minister in 1979. Clark's regime offered Alberta a choice opportunity to deal with a fellow Alberta Conservative over national energy policy, clearly determining the split in revenues between Alberta and the feds. Within a few months, an energy "summit" occurred between Lougheed and Clark and their ministers to reach a lasting deal. Lougheed was fresh back in Edmonton from that summit in Saskatoon as martinis arrived for our repast.

Lougheed was dripping with contempt for Clark. By his account, the Alberta contingent arrived with thorough briefing papers and proposals on energy, aiming for a quick and solid resolution. Clark arrived with almost no one else, nothing prepared, and very little understanding of the issues. Within a day, said Lougheed, it was clear that Ottawa was entirely out of its depth and incapable of making any kind of commitments on energy anytime soon. He regarded Clark as woefully jejune for his responsibilities as prime minister.

Such conversations influenced our coverage, to be sure. But the effect was limited. Clark bungled his way out of his minority government that December, and by February 1980, Pierre Trudeau was PM again in a Second Coming, saying, "Welcome to the '80s." It would be a raucous four years in federal-provincial relations and a great time to be associate editor of the Edmonton Journal.

***

Monty was ambivalent about living with me from the outset. We went back and forth between commitment and rejection, somewhat more commitment on my side, perhaps. This showed up in the spring of 1978 in an interesting way.

He loved dogs, as did I. I suggested we get a puppy. He opposed that idea with an unusual objection: It would suggest our relationship had a future, which would be unfair to the puppy.

We had earlier discussed Olde English Sheepdogs. In June, I checked the ads and found one such male puppy available at a farm/kennel just outside of town, a purebred imported from Kansas, some 10 weeks old. One lovely evening that week, I suggested we go for a drive in the country. We came upon a farmhouse, and I headed up the driveway. Monty quickly expressed alarm that we

201

were trespassing. At the house was a sign describing a kennel.

Monty refused to get out of the car. I went in, and they showed me an adorable Sheepdog puppy in a box. I brought him outside, and he started running around. Monty emerged from the car, and the puppy ran straight at him. We took him home an hour later.

We named him Tye, and he became a beloved presence in our household. At the same time, Monty insisted that Tye was my dog, not his, to the point I had to buy Tye's food separately and pay his vet bills myself. But the really passionate relationship in that house was between Tye and Monty. They were the real lovers.

When Monty and I split four years later, I knew Tye had to go with him – the primary link. Monty was deeply happy with that, and years later, when Tye died in Vancouver, Monty sent a beautiful card with Tye's picture and a note of thanks. Tye's ashes rest under Monty's bed in Vancouver. He never got another dog.

A year later, living alone, I decided to get another puppy and returned to that same kennel. I got an Airedale and took him home on a Saturday afternoon. Sunday afternoon, I returned him to the kennel, realizing I was on the cusp of leaving Edmonton and could not provide a proper home. I liked to say that "a dog is not a thing; it is a relationship." I wasn't prepared for another one just then.

In Toronto, I never got a dog because I was too busy to be a good partner (maybe for humans too). Now I share two dogs at my seasonal house in Costa Rica, and they are very much relationships. In the eight months I am not there, they are surrounded by staff and friends. In the four months that I am there, we are family.

***

I got back to writing music for the Walterdale Theatre melodrama each summer at the Citadel Theatre. I accompanied the performance on the piano from the pit and wrote the individual show tunes for the "stars." We sold out 700 seats a night for two weeks in July. Earlier, I had connected with three women friends to create a music group called "Thor and the Roses," featuring the American songbook, me on the piano, they in three-part harmony. We performed at parties and weddings and even a downtown jazz club, the Yardbird Suite. Music was and remains a central part of my experience.

***

In 1981, I had a hankering for a more commodious house. I had paid $32,000 for my little gem on the bank of the North Saskatchewan River in Skunk Hollow in 1975. I sold it for $123,000 and bought an elegant mid-century bungalow in an upscale neighbourhood in the west end. Monty and I made the house over, and it emerged as elegant indeed. But times were getting itchy.

***

Pierre Trudeau's last term as prime minister was nirvana for journalism in Alberta. The National Energy Program was a frontal attack on Alberta's rights and interests. The proposed patriation of the Constitution, including a Charter of Rights and Freedoms and amending formula, was fraught with implications. Responsible for the Journal's editorial voice on all this, I was intensely engaged, learned much, and perhaps made some contribution to various outcomes.

Meanwhile, CBC radio called, and I became a frequent contributor to As It Happens, hosted by Barbara Frum. We got to know each other on-air long before she became a friend with her husband Murray in Toronto. I also became a bi-weekly "Alberta columnist" with Alberta Report publisher Ted Byfield on Peter Gzowski's "Morningside." (Byfield was writing a book on the clash of civilizations between Christianity and Islam, which I thought was a totally academic sidebar.) Alberta was central to Canadian issues then, and I was at the centre of analytical journalism in Edmonton. This final return to the city of my youth was turning out rather well, in fact.

The Edmonton Journal sided completely with Lougheed on the NEP, and he was not happy when we suggested he had come out second-best in his eventual agreement with Trudeau on the issues. (Lougheed always regretted the photo of him and Trudeau raising champagne glasses to toast the truce.) More importantly, we kept in close touch with Lougheed on the constitutional package, where Lougheed played a critical role in devising the amending formula for the Constitution. The "7-50" formula with a Notwithstanding clause had its genesis in Edmonton (and Regina with Premier Allan Blakeney). And Edmonton mayor Laurence Decore, of Ukrainian heritage, played a big role in getting multiculturalism inserted into the Charter of Rights.

Finally, on TV, I watched Queen Elizabeth sign the new constitutional agreements into law on a rainy Ottawa Saturday, April 17, 1982. The Constitution Act, 1982 was now in force.

The following Monday morning, there was a ruckus down the hall at the publisher's office at the Edmonton

Journal. Agents from Ottawa's Competition Bureau were confiscating files from Patrick's office, looking for evidence that the Journal had engaged in anti-competitive behaviour against the upstart Edmonton Sun, which had recently arrived in town from Toronto. The Feds had boxes of the publisher's files piling up on the floor.

Our lawyers rushed over and asked the Feds: "Where is your search warrant?" The Ottawa guys replied that, under the Competition Act, they didn't require a search warrant. And our guys replied that under the Charter of Rights and Freedoms, which had come into effect two days earlier, they did. The Charter provided protection against "unreasonable search and seizure," which applied to all federal legislation. A quick visit to the courts downtown led a somewhat perplexed judge to freeze the files pending review.

Thus, within 48 hours, we launched the first-ever challenge to federal law under the Charter of Rights and Freedoms, a case known as Southam vs. Hunter, which we ultimately won. The Competition Bureau would now need search warrants to raid private property. This experience would play a big part a few years later when I wrote a series of editorials at The Globe and Mail regarding search warrants that won me a National Newspaper Award and, as part of a reporting team, the Michener Award for Public Service Journalism. I subsequently launched several "free speech" challenges to federal laws under the charter myself, as editor-in-chief of The Globe and Mail. I had learned much along the way.

***

I became friends with Mel Hurtig during these seven years in Edmonton, a man of warmth, high self-regard and intelligence. He and his lady would come to our house in Skunk Hollow for dinner and later to our house in the west end. And frequently, he would ask me over for martinis at 5 pm at his penthouse overlooking the Saskatchewan River valley (the entry door made of steel for his security). He made the martinis secretively in the kitchen to conceal his recipe and brought them out with some flair. Then we would do it again. I learned much later that the secret to his recipe was the addition of a drop of scotch. The other secret was they were doubles, and we had two.

I had bought a sleek 1972 Jaguar sedan, which I saw in a used car lot and could not resist. Six months later, Mel asked me for lunch at the Mayfair Golf Club (which once prohibited Jews), where he proposed that I be the editor of the Canadian Encyclopedia, for which he had won government funds. Also present was his current lady friend, Barbara Kelly. I deferred on the encyclopedia, preferring daily journalism to years in the stacks. As we were saying goodbye in the parking lot, Barbara suddenly exclaimed, "Mel – look at that fabulous car – my favourite in the whole world!" I ambled over, opened the door and said, "Would you like to take it for a drive?"

I had just put it up for sale, daunted by the continuing stream of expensive repairs it demanded. Mel took it for a week and had it assessed at the local dealer. I sold it to him for the same price I had paid six months earlier. Years later, Mel warned everyone about the used-car salesmen that was William, having poured countless thousands of dollars more into the elegant beast.

I visited Mel whenever I returned to Edmonton later, and have a photo of us in front of his fireplace at Christmas, toasting each other with martinis. He writes on it: "The Really Odd Couple enjoying the only thing they have in common."

We actually had much in common, but subsequently had some difficult encounters over political stuff, and I will always miss his company.

***

Barbara Frum was coming to Edmonton on CBC business and invited me to dinner at a restaurant with some colleagues. This was our first in-person meeting, having spoken many times on-air through "As It Happens." I noticed she did not shake her right hand. (We never discussed, in all the subsequent years of our friendship, her challenging health status.) We had a lively conversation. She said she had been asked to leave CBC Radio for a new CBC TV news program at night, but was unsure. I encouraged her to make the move to television, my opinion being, I am sure, inconsequential.

Many months later, I was on the Edmonton Journal business in Toronto, and Barbara invited me to be in the studio while she hosted The Journal – CBC TV's new flagship public affairs program after the national news at 10. At its conclusion, we boarded a limo waiting for her on Jarvis Street and went up to her house for dinner. That is where I met Murray Frum in an amazing space filled with art. We had Chinese take-out. It was excellent, and I knew I had to get back to Toronto.

***

Patrick O'Callaghan announced he was leaving the Edmonton Journal to become publisher of the Calgary

Herald. We mourned his transfer as our champion, not only in Edmonton but within Southam. Patrick was fiercely independent as the publisher of the Journal, which was sending millions of dollars to Toronto's head office from our profits. He told me once that a vice-president of Southam had shown up unannounced at our front door, and the receptionist called up to Patrick's office to notify him. Patrick replied that the guy didn't have an appointment and should return to Toronto to make one. Which he did.

Patrick called from Calgary a month later and said he wanted me to come down as editor of the Calgary Herald. Naturally, I said yes. (When I told my mother, she replied typically, "That's nice.") Monty and I visited Calgary to look for a house and found two candidate properties in Mount Royal. We returned to our hotel to weigh the merits, sipping wine and gazing out over the city, imaging the future. I was suddenly struck by a "truth." I was keen to leave Edmonton after five or six years and also depressed at the thought of staying in Alberta. If I came to Calgary, I might be there the rest of my career. To Monty's relief, I announced that we would not be moving to Calgary.

I told Patrick, with great apologies, and he was not happy. He was Irish and took these things to heart – as a betrayal. In subsequent years, we were on good terms, but always with an edge.

I told Southam I wanted to move, either to our Ottawa or Vancouver papers, preferably Ottawa, where I proposed to vastly strengthen the Citizen as a national capital newspaper, incorporating the Southam national news bureau on the lines of the Washington Post. Neither bid bore fruit. (I had a cool relationship with Patrick's successor as publisher in Edmonton, a person whom I thought tried to buy gratitude through excessive generosity when he could not earn respect.)

The Globe and Mail's Edmonton correspondent, Jeff Sallot, was a friend with his wife Rosemary Boyle, who worked at CBC. He called to say the new editor-in-chief of The Globe and Mail was coming through town as part of a bureau tour. Could we have lunch?

Norman Webster was delightful and humane, with a sharp eye for bullshit. Within a few weeks, I agreed to return to the Editorial Board of The Globe and Mail at a significant pay cut after seven years away and to cover my own moving expenses this time. It was spring 1984, and I would have to sell my house at a loss and head east without a car – all worth the investment, I was sure. Two weeks later, Mel Hurtig took me to watch the Edmonton Oilers win their first Stanley Cup.

***

Monty and I had split a year earlier, drifting into separate worlds. He was aiming for Vancouver and said, "William, Toronto is a producer city, and Vancouver is a consumer city. You are a producer, and I am a consumer." There was some truth to that. He then said that he envied my next boyfriend. "Why?" I asked. "Because you have learned so much from me." He was right about that too, and I had also learned more about me from myself. We remain friendly.

Some months later, I met a guy at Flashback whom I found hopelessly attractive. He was a medical student visiting from Germany, and we spent five eventful days together over the Labour Day long weekend. When I returned home from leaving him at the airport and went to bed, I found under my pillow a sprig of twigs and dried flowers from our walks in the valley. Norbert asked about my new place in Toronto a year later, and we planned a reunion there. He died of AIDS soon after.

I sold my big Edmonton house during the recession of 1984, bought a little house in Toronto's Moore Park, and arrived there in early August, thrilled to be back at

The Globe and Mail and in the city. From my last column in the Edmonton Journal, July 1984:

"When I return to visit my family [in Alberta]... I want to see inventiveness take the place of luck. I want to see strategy take the place of grievance. I want to see 'yes' rise up more often to meet the yawning possibilities."

Who knew what might happen next?

***

TORONTO: THE GLOBE AND MAIL

I turned 39 as I landed in Toronto and dived into the gay scene with relish. The bars were lively, and by chance, just down the street from me was Toronto's major gay cruising spot, David Balfour Park. These years were filled with encounters and adventures, but few led to any serious stuff. By my late '40s, I started to think I might remain single and would have to manage it. So it was to be.

***

The Globe and Mail newsroom at 444 Front Street W. was as ratty and cramped as I remembered. Most of the reporters and editors dressed out of Eddie Bauer - cargo pants, flannel shirts and loose things in various shades of brown. I wore a white shirt and tie every day with proper slacks, as the editorial board often met with important visitors and besides, it was the editorial board. I loved this reunion with The Globe.

Editor-in-chief Norman Webster chaired the board with intelligence and grace, calling upon our individual expertise to select and define the issues. I covered national policy, including politics, economics, law and the arts, and produced one of four "leaders" a day at around 900 words. My colleagues were smart and affable, and we made a strong team. Soon, people were commenting on the rising force of The Globe's editorials, due really to Norman's leadership at the board. We got a full-page photo in Toronto Life magazine.

Dic Doyle was editor emeritus, writing a column from an office beside the publisher. It was warming to see him again, and we sometimes went to lunch. I did not much like his appointment soon after to the Senate by Brian Mulroney, however: It seemed like a belated conflict of interest, though Dic did make a good Senator.

Within weeks of my arrival in September 1984, Brian Mulroney's Progressive Conservatives won a huge majority in Ottawa, and the Macdonald Commission emerged with a recommendation that Canada seeks free trade with the United States. Norman Webster wrote the editorial endorsing Mulroney, and it soon fell to me to become our voice in support of free trade and deregulation within the federal sphere in Canada. I was also responsible for national politics, including federal finances. (My editorial on Michael Wilson's first budget in 1985 titled: "Mr. Wilson Disappoints," the first of many such in the Mulroney years.) In the newsroom, which had a good contingent of left-leaning journalists, I was soon typed as the preppy right-wing Albertan with a tie, dubiously giving The Globe a rather louder, more consistent conservative voice.

A year later, the editor of our monthly Report on Business Magazine asked me to write a business-book review at some 1,200 words at the back of each issue. Peter Cook was an elegant Brit and our leading business columnist as well. I wrote those reviews for the next several years, including a rather prescient one on Donald Trump's Art of the Deal in June 1988, which gave me some profile beyond the anonymity of the editorial board: "New York billionaire real estate developer Donald Trump has written a banal, engaging and self-serving autobiography filled with many opinions and nary one idea. The man is inventive, conceited, pugnacious and may run for public office. If elected, he will not serve but rather lead in feudal style. If defeated, he will not grimace but rather claim that victory would have driven him mad by depriving him of independence." We will see.

I was paired at the back of the magazine with Conrad Black, whose columns were invariably informed and entertaining. I saw him standing alone at a Canadian Press reception and introduced myself as his ROB writing partner. We became friends and remain so, though his writings now divert for more troubling reasons.

In 1986, the Premiers came up with the "Edmonton Declaration," laying out a series of constitutional goals intended to win Quebec's belated signature to the Constitution Act of 1982. This became the Meech Lake Accord in the spring of 1987, giving Ottawa and all provincial governments three years to ratify it. This, too, became my file on the editorial board, along with free trade. It was a wonderful assignment, intense and polarizing. Canada's leading constitutional scholar, Peter Hogg, became my generous mentor on the phone.

Barbara Frum called up often to probe some aspect of the free trade agreement or Meech Lake accord she would be discussing that night on The Journal. I became part of her always thorough research network, and we took to one-hour phone conversations most Saturday mornings to review events. She didn't answer one Saturday in March 1992; I spoke at her memorial service in Massey Hall.

***

I renovated my little house on Moore Avenue (at one point down to $260 in the bank), created a deck and garden, and hosted many parties there. My mother Irene sent money to buy a car in December 1984 and visited the next summer with my sister Corinne. One year later, she returned with my Aunt Bobbie, and they insisted on staying in a hotel to enjoy the city-centre lifestyle. After a lively family dinner at my house, I prepared to drive them downtown when my mother said, "Oh, no, I'll just walk home." Bobbie reminded her they were in Toronto, not Edmonton. This was the first distinct sign of my mother's incipient Alzheimer's disease that would command the end of her life for a decade (then Bobbie's too).

In the early 1990s, I would visit Irene in Edmonton, where my sister Corinne was managing her care at home. Women from Chile (Ruth Herrera) and Guatemala moved in and lived with my mother until she died in 1996 – they were her last, excellent family. I learned to call my mother by her name – Irene – rather than mom because she was losing her memory, sequentially from the present, and she wasn't a mom yet in, say, 1935. I started by asking what she was up to that day, and she recalled bringing in wood for the stove in New Norway or going to a piano lesson. (Oh, it must be about 1925.) Then we could have a conversation. Eventually, no specific memory remained, so I would put on a favourite record, and she would smile and clutch my hand.

Through all this, Corinne managed everything, an enormous, loving contribution to Irene and to my brother Jim and father Arne, who, like me, were living away.

***

In November 1988, Brian Mulroney was re-elected prime minister in a political battle that was all about free trade – yes or no. We had fervently supported him editorially in the name of free trade, an agreement reached with the United States in 1987, and which the Canadian Senate would not approve without a federal election. (I explained to a convention of Americans downtown that, given Canada's parliamentary system with three main parties, Mulroney needed only about 43 percent of the popular vote to command a majority in Parliament: In sum, we were hoping for a big enough minority of voters to ram free trade through over the majority of voters – a virtue of the parliamentary system in my view. The audience was appalled.)

I was in the newsroom watching the results on TV, where Mulroney had just got his majority of seats. Our publisher, Roy Megarry, came up and asked how I felt. I said, "I much prefer to win," and rushed off to finish that night's editorial. I drove home up Mt. Pleasant Road at 3 am in fresh snow, deeply content.

Two weeks later, at my year-end interview with Norman Webster, he said they were thinking of creating a new position: editor of the opinion pages – the role I had played in Edmonton more than four years earlier. He said they had me in mind, and I said, great. We would come back to it in the new year.

Just before Christmas, Norman told us he was stepping down as editor-in-chief and would take a year's sabbatical before returning to write a column – a huge and disconcerting surprise. For the next three weeks, we all went to work without Norman in the building and no further information. (Norman and the managing editor, Geoffrey Stevens, had left for a month-long tour of our foreign bureaus.) The publisher was also abroad and silent. We all wondered what was next: Then the phone rang at my home on Moore Avenue.

***

It was the first Saturday in January 1989, and I went to St. Lawrence Market to buy stuff for a dinner party I was hosting that evening for friends, including Peggy Wente, who was now editor of Report on Business Magazine, having succeeded Peter Cook in 1986.

Peter had a party at his house in North Toronto to welcome Peggy to The Globe on a warm summer night in 1986. I was writing my monthly book review in the magazine, so Peggy would now be my editor there. We swanned around Peter's swimming pool and had a good time. My own career as an editor would twine through with Peggy's in time.

Some weeks before that party, I had met Philip walking through David Balfour Park on Saturday afternoon. He was wearing a striped blue and white jersey, which looked very good from the back. I followed him up a path, and then he followed me home. He was in his final year as a BA student at the University of Toronto. And he was smart and sexy.

On the Saturday evening of Peter's party for Peggy, Philip and I wanted to be together. I left the front door of my house unlocked and said he should come over whenever he could and I would be home after 11 pm. When I returned to the dark house, his jacket was hanging in the hall. When I crawled into bed, his feet were still cold from walking over, and he refused to go to sleep. Our boy-boy story would become more complex and significant in the years to come.

***

I had just arrived home from the market on that first Saturday in January 1989 when the phone rang. To my amazement, it was Roy Megarry, fresh back from Peru over Christmas, where he supported a significant development project. He asked how things were going in the newsroom, and I replied that we were fine and wanted more information about recent events. He asked whether I could come in for tea the next afternoon – Sunday – and I said sure. I would be there in any case to write my column for ROB Magazine.

My dinner party that evening was filled with speculation and gossip about the dramatic changes at The Globe. I said nothing about Roy's call. I sensed that Peggy's antennae were high.

The next morning, I sat at my messy dining room table and composed a short list of observations about The Globe, sensing that Roy was planning to discuss the new role as editor of the opinion pages raised by Norman Webster a month before. Then I went in for tea.

***

EDITOR-IN-CHIEF, THE GLOBE AND MAIL

Photo Credit, Ed Lum

I think neither Roy nor myself foresaw what was to unfold that afternoon. Between 2 pm and 5 pm, we became engrossed in a conversation about The Globe and journalism in general, requiring a second pot of tea as darkness fell. At one point, Roy reached into his pocket and laid a piece of paper on the coffee table, saying he wanted to make a few observations about The Globe in its present state. I asked whether I could precede him just to assert an independent view. Certainly, he replied.

I acknowledged the newspaper's many virtues, then described where improvements were possible, not just in my view, but among some of my peers. Among them were the paper's graphic design and organization and its hewing to traditional definitions of "news." I suggested that opinion columns should range more widely beyond policy questions into social and cultural matters. As I finished up, Roy said he would make yet another pot of tea.

We discussed each of my points for the next hour or so, Roy added more, and I saw him slyly remove his piece of paper from the table and return it to his pocket. It was now dark outside at 5 pm, and I made a move to leave. Roy stood up and said: "I have just found my next editor-in-chief." I think I looked over my shoulder. It was a complete surprise to me and, I am quite sure, to him.

I had no time to do anything but assent in a state of excited disequilibrium. Roy went to the phone, called his wife and said, "I have just found my next editor-in-chief." I knew Barbara, and she was apparently happy with the news. Roy said we would make the announcement the next afternoon.

Then, as we were leaving, I thought, "oops." I stopped and said to Roy, you have to know that I am gay, and I will not stop being gay if I play this new role. If that is a problem, we can leave this aside. He replied that the whole newsroom knew I was gay and that if any problem ever came up about that fact, he'd have my back. Besides, I was single and would be able to work long hours indeed! We shook hands, and I headed into the night.

***

I went to visit close friends to share this. They were out at a movie. Overnight, I became filled with doubts and questions about this dramatic change. I was waiting for Roy when he arrived in the morning and said I wanted to have lunch with my colleague Peter Cook before officially signing on. Roy was visibly surprised and said OK. I shared the news with Peter, who was immediately encouraging and said most other people would be too. I returned and said to Roy, full steam ahead. He introduced me to Diane Barsoski, the head of human resources, and they reiterated their support of me being gay, assuming that was what had given me pause. It wasn't, but I appreciated it deeply.

Roy made the announcement in the newsroom that afternoon to much amazement, some joy and no little incredulity. I quickly realized that most everyone wanted to know why me? Why was I hired? Norman Webster and

Geoffrey Stevens were abroad and would not return for another three weeks.

I told Roy I wanted to give a talk to the newsroom, summarizing our conversation on Sunday – what I said and what he said. Transparency was essential to clear the air. He agreed. Two days later, the whole newsroom was there in the early afternoon, with bureaus on the phone lines and TV cameras waiting outside. Why was I hired? I said this was a summary of my conversation with Roy on Sunday afternoon as Roy stood at the back of the room. We were headed for a major redesign and a shift in the nature of our journalism to less institutional reporting, more explanatory reporting, and new species of content entirely. Pretty general, but more to come. That's it, I concluded: There is nothing more behind the curtain.

Except for one thing.

I had said to Roy on Sunday that my chances of bringing about major changes would be enhanced, I thought, with the appointment of a new managing editor. Geoffrey Stevens was very good, as far as I knew, and was travelling abroad with Norman Webster until the end of January. But I had a sense that I would face resistance to many of my rather radical ideas from that essential office if he remained in place. (Why? I just felt it – a not very convincing answer, to be sure, and Geoffrey was nowhere near.) Roy said it was my call, and I made it that first afternoon. Geoffrey had been a stellar national columnist for some years in Ottawa, and I wanted him to do the same thing for us in the United States – to be our de Tocqueville in understanding our most important foreign relationship. I would ask him to make the switch on his return on a Friday at the end of the month; I practiced my lines. I urged that he take whatever time to consider this or other options with the paper. I wanted him on board.

On Sunday, two days after our discussion, both he and Norman Webster cleared out their offices and quit the newspaper, Geoffrey later suing the publisher for allegedly breaking an earlier commitment that he would stay on as managing editor under any new editor-in-chief. (He won a settlement.) Just back from their world tour of the bureaus, Norman and Geoffrey gave me no news of this during a rather dark staff party on that Saturday night. We never had a conversation about any of this.

So I came home from Sunday afternoon in the country with my house-guest Anne Wheeler to find my phone answering machine overloaded: Norman and Geoffrey had quit The Globe and Mail that afternoon and left the building. There would be no names on the masthead for Monday's edition (they had removed their names with two days left in their official tenure). I drove right down to Front Street and put my name up there on the masthead, where it needed to be. The newsroom was roiled, to be sure, tears here and there. Two of the most respected journalists in Canada were gone from The Globe and Mail in a day with no precise explanation of why.

(Almost 20 years later, Norman Webster called, and we had a friendly lunch at the ROM's new C5 restaurant on the roof. We exchanged not a word about The Globe and Mail. I much admired him when we worked together and appreciated his discreet silence about The Globe after he left. I never had a subsequent conversation with Geoffrey Stevens.)

It was tumultuous and challenging as I took the Editor's chair. I was surprised and sobered by this experience, having alienated two people I respected very much and no doubt many more. I reflected on the wisdom of my decisions, but it was done and gone, and they had made theirs. I had an enormous agenda now and could face only one direction – forward. I would be in that chair the better part of eleven years.

***

Roy sent me home with a stack of black, numbered binders stamped "Confidential" – financial and business data about The Globe and Mail. We were modestly profitable, with a circulation of around 330,000 weekdays and 300,000 Saturdays. We had targets for revenue, profitability and circulation for December 1989, twelve months hence. It was pretty straightforward.

Returning all to Roy, I said I found the data interesting, as we in the newsroom were always speculating about such numbers. I asked why all this was confidential. Why could we not share it with the staff? Was there some competitive reason not to do so? A couple of days later, he came to say that confidentiality was simply a tradition, and there was no reason not to share it.

Thus began my monthly "Notes from the Overground" memo to the newsroom that laid out our financial and circulation goals (including the target rate of return on revenue), the size and distribution of the newsroom budget, and how we were doing each month, among many other things. These monthly missives quickly vaporized many conspiracy theories about Thomson Corp., bleeding us dry (on the contrary) or the

229

supposedly favoured status of this or that department in the newsroom. Over time, I found many of my editorial colleagues taking pride in meeting our business goals, and this flow of information ultimately contributed to much better relations with our unions across the paper.

Roy then shared a memo he had written to Norman Webster in the fall of 1988, listing various things Roy thought needed attention, changes to be made and such. It included Norman's generally cooperative reply. I read it and responded to Roy that it was obviously relevant information, but it was not addressed to me. I would take or leave from it. (One thing I would not do is dismiss June Callwood as a freelance columnist. She resigned sometime later in the face of my uncomfortable silence. Several staff writers also resigned to go elsewhere, assuming I was a hostile force.)

A few days after I took the chair, I got a call from Prime Minister Brian Mulroney, whom I had not met. He wished me well and said I might learn from the mistakes he had made in his first term. I replied that I had documented all of them personally and publicly as an editorial writer and felt much wiser already from his volatile experience. And so began a relationship that grew into some significance as the years came on.

Barbara and Murray Frum were good friends and invited me to dinner at their amazing home a few weeks later. I arrived to find no parking spaces on the street for a block or so and thought someone must be having a party. When I came to their door, I saw Conrad Black through the glass and a great crowd beyond. The Frums had cleared out their living room for dining tables, and Mardi Gras decorations abounded. "Le tout" Toronto was there to mark my appointment, together with the presence of Marcel Masse, federal Minister of Communications. I responded to a toast as best I could, and in my note of thanks to them, said, "I only hope I do not let you down."

***

Within six months, I learned that the annual "churn" on our subscriptions was 44 percent, a number I found high and almost insulting. (Almost half our subscribers did not renew their subscriptions.) I learned that the average reader spent 17 minutes a day reading The Globe, a number that I found low and almost insulting. Discussions with Roy led to a radical innovation. He included both the rate of churn in subscriptions and the average time reading The Globe in my bonus calculations. And to make that meaningful, he gave me responsibility for circulation strategy and marketing as

Head of a new Reader Development Group, with a staff of three researchers led by Nigel Pleasance. (Apparently, I was the first editor of a major paper in North America to have these additional responsibilities.) This precocious group went on to wreak something of a revolution in how to think about circulation beyond the realm of editorial content itself.

At our year-end management meeting in 1989, Roy said our circulation target would increase as usual by 2 percent in 1990. Knowing that we sold the physical paper at a loss to most readers (paper, ink and distribution), I asked why we would do that: Could we raise cover prices, ad rates or find new advertisers to cover the cost? Absolutely not, said the relevant managers. So why increase circulation? "Rare question," said Roy. It was a system-wide policy at Thomson Newspapers; maybe we should do more work on it.

In August 1990, my Reader Development Group produced a document called "Ideal Circulation" for The Globe and Mail. The analysis was based on advertiser needs, Globe demographics and the economics of selling the paper across Canada through various channels. In summary, we concluded:

* Our daily circulation should focus even more strongly on major urban centres with a higher

proportion of managers, owners and professionals (MOPES) in the mix. We should shed expensive circulation in rural and some regional markets with "unfavourable" demographics. (It's called focus.)

* This done, our weekday circulation should fall from 330,000 to 317,000, giving better value to advertisers and less cost to ourselves. (It's called productivity.)

* We should drastically reduce sales through expensive street boxes and concentrate on subscriptions, single-copy sales in stores, and corporate sales (hotels, airlines). And we should move aggressively to monthly billing for subscriptions using credit cards or bank withdrawals as one means to lower churn. (It's called strategy.)

Roy and the management committee embraced this report, and we set out to implement it, initially over the objection of Thomson Newspapers, which couldn't believe that any paper would set out to reduce its circulation. Together with our editorial redesign in June 1990 and changes in content that supported higher cover prices, we substantially improved the economics of circulation, adding millions annually to the bottom line. (Our renewal rate at higher subscription and price levels increased from 56 percent to 74 percent in five years.)

A few weeks after my appointment as editor-in-chief, we had a meeting of the management committee – the heads of advertising, circulation, finance, marketing, HR and such. Roy was out of town. The head of HR and the guy responsible for marketing took me aside and said I should expect a three-year run in Roy's good books. He would grow impatient and move on. They said, "Use your window well." I was taken aback by their candour and doubted their thesis, but kept the memory tight of that conversation.

In December 1989, I sat with Roy for my first year-end review. At some point, he asked what had been my biggest surprise in the chair so far: "Malice," I said, "the degree of malice toward me among some in the newsroom, whom I had never directly offended." Offended loyalties were surely in play, but other causes would emerge.

He asked what my biggest mistakes had been so far. I came up with a few, but they didn't loom very large. "That's the problem," he said. "You haven't made any big mistakes yet, because you haven't taken any significant risks. You came into the job with big plans for change, but not much has happened in 10 months." I thought that was a fair observation and said I had been gearing up and he would see a great deal more change in 1990. Then I asked what my budget for big mistakes was – how many of them and how big before I saw the door? We laughed, and he said that particular budget was a secret.

In subsequent months and years, several senior editors departed The Globe, claiming to represent others who feared for the paper under my leadership. (Unforgivably, I had never been a beat reporter and, I learned much later, had been described with alarm as the "gay Norwegian" from Alberta at the head of Canada's National Newspaper!) One day, Roy reported he had just had lunch in his dining room with a person we both knew (not working at The Globe), who argued the same point: I should not be editor-in-chief, and he was willing to fill the void. Roy said: "William, I will never allow that man to enter this building again, and neither should you." And so it was. I rather loved Roy Megarry for that alone.

***

On my appointment in January 1989, I received a letter from a psychologist friend who had worked for various government agencies and boards. She said from what she knew of me, I was quite unprepared for the dangers of office politics at the top " –naïve" was her word. She went into detail about the dynamics of power around any CEO, starting with the "fact" that every CEO has mortal enemies within the organization, not because of his or her actions, but simply because the CEO had the job they desired. She talked about building a core group of loyalists, of identifying the anonymous plotters who might be very close to you, and of creating some kind of feedback and intelligence network to avoid dangerous isolation in the corner suite. Read Shakespeare!

I thought most of this to be melodramatic, but it was true that, since Expo 67, I had not been in senior management in a meaningful sense for any period of time, and never at The Globe. I was a writer who worked with a few colleagues and mostly alone. My experience over the next decade would teach me much more about the dangers my friend described, and I had to pay attention or risk my career. At the same time, I had to develop much more effective leadership skills or risk my career. There were some close calls along the way, and I rarely let anyone know how much I knew about some mutinous matters involving them. Survival was a much bigger part of the job than I had realized – and the condition of making all the changes in editorial content I now set out to do.

***

I had promised Roy a complete redesign and reorganization of the paper, together with new approaches to our journalism. I needed a compatible Design Director to execute the first part and finally found Tony Sutton, a Brit who had been working in South Africa. He knew the ropes and was prepared to follow my lead. I wanted a high-class graphic presentation, clean and communicative at the same time. We set to work in January 1990.

Meanwhile, I was shifting beat reporting away from institutional coverage – i.e. school boards – to coverage on the ground – what is happening in the actual classrooms of the nation? The labour beat became the workplace beat, too much consternation among some reporters who saw the shift from covering labour unions to including the actual workplace as a right-wing plot. We created beats on multiculturalism to probe the fact of our quickly diversifying cities and Social Trends to document wider evolution in the culture. We created our first foreign "beat" assignment – Development Issues – based in India, not to cover a country, rather the dynamics of development in many countries: Why and how did it work and not work? We brought this approach to Report on Business (Amazing Facts, The Change Page), News (Middle Kingdom), the Arts and Sport (Truth and

Rumours; the Game/Story). This would evolve as the years passed, and many reporters bloomed in these new assignments.

I described this new "process" take on journalism in the Clissold Lecture at the University of Western Ontario in the spring of 1990. Thomson Newspapers printed that lecture and sent it to almost 200 newspapers in Britain and the United States. (I shared it with Neil Postman in New York, author of "Amusing Ourselves to Death," whom I had come to know and who heartily endorsed it.) The headline on the Thomson reprint was "Yesterday's News Is No Longer Fit to Print" – not so popular with the journalism establishment and many in my newsroom. It was something of my charter of journalism for The Globe and Mail as editor-in-chief, from which:

"The most disconcerting thing for North American newspapers these days is that a smaller proportion of ageing Canadians and Americans is reading them, and this smaller proportion is reading them less intensely.... By measures of ubiquity, loyalty and perhaps even respect, newspapers do not appear to hold the place they once did in North American society. This is not necessarily a terrible thing for society, though most newspaper people think it is...

"Newspapers require considerable time, effort and privacy to read about bureaucratic, complicated and often depressing situations over which readers feel they have little control and may, in any case, be losing interest. Many fine journalists do an excellent job of describing the complexities and problems of modern life, but many former and potential readers apparently no longer want journalistic excellence in that garb. And this is one of the saddest things about modern newsrooms: Good people doing good work are facing declining public interest in their undoubted skills and achievements...

"The five W's of reporting (what, who, where, when and why) are heavy on description. I believe the five Ws must be supplemented by the capital-H of *How* and the capital-SW of *So-What*. How do things work? How do things happen? Why does it matter?

"The classic definition of news can be summarized, I think, as 'what went wrong yesterday.' ... The traditional definition of news has made very little room for 'what went RIGHT yesterday 'except in the fields of medicine and science, where advances are usually hot stuff on our front pages. We all know about the tragic problem of AIDS; does anyone doubt that a solution would be front-page news?

"What went right in educating high school students, what went right in reducing welfare cases, what went right in improving the efficiency of the hospital system, what went right in turning a struggling retail empire around does not qualify in the minds of most journalists as compelling news...

"When we speak so reverentially of investigative journalism, we mean uncovering something that has gone wrong – 'the wronger the better '– growing out of the classic but intellectually careless aphorism that it is the role of journalists 'to comfort the afflicted and afflict the comfortable. '(Why, in principle, would we want to afflict the comfortable?)... As a result, we tend to be somewhat like fundamentalist preachers in our concentration on the evils of the world, ponderously finger-wagging from page one right through columns, editorials and reviews...

"Newspapers are transfixed with what goes wrong to the point that the same features on familiar problems recycle themselves with numbing predictability year after year, newspaper after newspaper. And it becomes redundant and boring...

"Surely, uncovering things that go right should also be considered a valued form of investigative journalism.

If it's a question of social conscience or social mission – and these motivations pervade newsrooms – uncovering what WORKS in a field otherwise strewn with problems should have as much moral appeal as what doesn't. I believe The Globe and Mail can do more of this reporting well, for which there is significant latent demand and compelling social purpose...

"What matters has to go beyond what happened yesterday to what may happen tomorrow. The future must also take its place in the traditional hierarchy of news. The greatest scoop of all may be a story about something that hasn't yet occurred. We consistently miss these scoops in our love affair with yesterday...

"We have great difficulty talking about the future without slipping into futurism, which has a bad name because it is so often cheap and wrong. But the pace of change has accelerated to the point that the future arrives much earlier than it used to, often with stunning effect. In 20 years, the Japanese have virtually overturned the American auto industry. Suddenly the depleting ozone layer is affecting global health. The changing face of immigration holds significant portents for Canadian society....

"In sum, the news is no longer what went wrong yesterday. It is what is wrong, right and different about things that really matter across a wider board than we are used to, with an emphasis on *How* and *Why* and a clear eye to the future. News is a much bigger assignment than it used to be. Its purpose is evolving toward what you might call adult education – map-making in an increasingly complex landscape of issues and events....

"Canadians deserve a better national newspaper than The Globe and Mail is today or ever has been. Better in that it has a clearer sense of its own agenda for the news. Better in that it explains more competently the Hows and Whys of things that really matter. Better in that it has a broader sense of time, including the future. Better in that it expands its admirable investigatory instincts to include news about what is going right and how. Better in that, it deepens its roots across the country and around the world. Better in that, it serves as a more accessible forum for national conversation and debate among its readers. Better, ultimately, in that it educates and, yes, delights its readers in what it brings to their minds and emotions in the ancient and incomparable medium of ink on paper."

This was a longer version of what I had said to Roy Megarry on the fateful Sunday in 1989 when he hired me.

242

The Globe appeared in four sections that changed order and location depending on the day of the week. The editorial pages sat on pages six and seven, breaking upfront news. In the redesign, all this would morph into consistent arrangements, with Arts having a daily front, along with a report on Business and Sport "reading in from the back" of the Arts section. The fourth section was reserved for special reports, driven by advertising. (I emphasized Arts and Books, creating a Globe and Mail National Books Bestseller List based on a sophisticated sampling system and pressing for more reviews of non-fiction.)

I learned early on in our news meetings that there was often not much news of real interest on a particular day: What then to put on the front page? We were at the mercy of external events in creating most of our content, most of that shared with all other media – commodity news. I vowed to alter that balance and generate more original content of value to readers that were independent of external events and assured distinctive value against our competitors every day.

" We are not in the business of selling newspapers," opined Roy Megarry, "We are in the business of buying time." We were purchasers, not sellers – and this important mantra would become my own, as the price of our reader's time continued to rise as more two-income families worked long hours and commuted farther. I wanted more of their time, and we would have to buy it with considerably more value, by various means. I argued that our content arrived on a certain kind of truck – the "news story" – and we seemed to have only that kind of truck. We need a broader fleet of vehicles to deliver engaging, useful information of many more kinds.

The most notable example of this at the beginning was the "Facts & Arguments" page (title inspired by Moscow's new glasnost Argumenti y Fakti publication), which I placed on the back cover of the first section, following the relocated opinion pages there – a three-page anchor. Facts & Arguments settled into three features: an essay written by a reader on something of relevance to our demographic that was not typically "news" illustrated by a free-lance artist; a feature called "Social Studies" which offered tidbits from anywhere (the wisdom on the "walls of tenement halls" I said, echoing Simon and Garfunkle) that offered engaging insights into society; and a column (called Fifth Column) on themes of relevance to our readers (education, marketing, cities, religion). Some years later, provoked by Ken Thomson in discussions with me, we gave over the column to "Lives Lived," obituaries of ordinary people across the country as a form of social history. Facts & Arguments spoke to values and offered delight beyond the monopoly of the newsroom.

Facts & Arguments was conceived as a narcotic independent of the "news" and soon became a reader favourite. Riding the subway, I could see many copies of The Globe's front page held high because readers were reading the back page more intently. Add five minutes to the average reading time. (Penguin Books published a compilation of reader essays from Facts & Arguments in 2002.)

With Tony Sutton, I settled on clean typography with a virtual ban on "reverse" printing – white type showing through black ink – which I saw as down-market. We created overlines and underlines to give much more immediate context to our headlines, drawing the readers in. We brought consistency in style to all regular columns and features – something of a revolution at The Globe. And then came the matter of the nameplate.

The Globe and Mail nameplate had been classic newspaper gothic for almost 150 years, a la The New

York Times. To clearly signal changes in content, and particularly mission, I wanted a new one, and Roy agreed to this radical proposal. (Where did he find the faith?) I worked hard with Tony and his team to create one and wasn't getting far as the months ticked by. Finally, I hired external consultants in Toronto – Gottshalk and Ash – to work on a parallel track for this item alone.

Stuart Ash and his team worked with me at their offices in Yorkville, where we eventually came up with a contemporary-looking hand-drawn font for The Globe and Mail, over which in delicate Bembo type we spaced out "Canada's National Newspaper." I took the first print-out of that title home, and it hangs on my wall to this day, still the best version of what has slightly evolved. That nameplate now shines ebulliently over downtown Toronto at The Globe's new building on King Street East. (Now they can't take that away from me.)

We took our redesign proposals to the management committee in March 1990, various pages pinned up on walls for comparison against the existing paper. Six of the 12 people in that meeting were supportive. Five were seriously doubtful, saying it was all too radical for The Globe and would alienate many readers. That is when Roy Megarry said memorably: "Everyone can see the risks of change; few can see the risks in not changing. It is because The Globe is the gold standard in Canadian newspapers that we can afford to take risks others will not. They will follow." Then he asked: "William, when can you do it?" I chose Tuesday, June 12, to launch before the summer holidays, not wanting to languish until fall despite tight timing. Our marketing campaign soon appeared on billboards with a fuzzy image of an altered newspaper saying, "The 1990s. Now at Your Doorstep." (Without Roy Megarry's judgment and, indeed, courage, nothing of this could have been done.)

We presented the redesign to the Thomson family at their annual corporate meeting at Roy Thomson Hall in May – and they embraced it. Almost an afterthought, we held focus groups in Toronto on St. Clair Avenue one month before launch. As we left the studio that evening, our New York City consultant said: "You have a winner here." That was good to hear because, by then, the die was cast. (The space we used for that focus group is now the office of my dentist, a witness to entropy.)

I sat through many focus groups in subsequent years across Canada, not asking what should we do, rather how we are doing. "What should we do" was for us to divine – a point made repeatedly by Roy Megarry.

Fundamentally, the editor-in-chief or CEO must "know" where to go and how to get to a better place, informed and agile along the way. We needed to invent desire rather than rely on established tastes. I guess that is one take on leadership: Good management deals well with the present and is golden; good leadership identifies smart destinations and is essential.

***

With Roy Megarry, June 12, 1990. Photo credit: Ed Lum

The Globe and Mail's existing typographical design, layouts and organization were loose and disorganized. So was our use of the language. We had an old, thin Style

Guide for language usage, rarely used. I assigned Warren Clements and Sandy Macfarlane to come up with a new one (illustrated by our brilliant cartoonist Brian Gable), with reversion to Canadian spellings ("colour"), honorifics and accurate words for new countries, new products and new ideas. The new Style Book came to some 375 pages, and we ultimately sold 20,000 copies to our readers, strengthening our bond with them even as we made a few dollars.

We created a Graphic Style guide to support the new design, used by all the make-up editors and essential to consistency and discipline across the paper.

We reviewed and re-issued our ethical standards policy to cover such things as conflicts of interest, anonymous sources and plagiarism. (We were resistant to anonymous sources, which now dominate news coverage in North America.)

I wanted to create manuals of standards, high, clear and particular to The Globe and Mail as measures of performance and, as importantly, sources of pride in working at Canada's National Newspaper.

Meanwhile, I met with our lawyers (Peter Jacobsen and Bruce MacDougall) and said I was not interested in fighting justified lawsuits for defamation. Once the facts were established, we would either defend ourselves fiercely or retract and apologize, however painful to our name, reporters and editors. I put it to the newsroom that we had enormous power to damage individuals through publication and ethical responsibility to use it well. As the big boy on the media block, it was no sign of weakness to acknowledge missteps. On the contrary, we had had too many avoidable accidents.

On the other hand, faced with febrile lawsuits intended to intimidate us, I warned their lawyers to recall Oscar Wilde's sad experience: The Globe would be deeply-sourced and relentless at cross-examination. Beware our cross-examination, I muttered darkly. This usually shut silly things down after they went home and read up on Oscar Wilde.

That meant, too, that I was on guard against stories that would invite justified lawsuits, and I spiked a few to distress among some editors. They would retire to lick their wounds with the tribe, and it did not always serve me well in the newsroom. Investigative journalism was a core part of our mandate and required disciplined execution to qualify for publication in The Globe. The scent in the hunt can sometimes prevail over the facts on the ground. I learned to be observant about that.

With Peter and Bruce, I also launched several important lawsuits in defence of free speech and freedom of the press against the federal government. I enjoyed these jousts and occasional skirmishes, too, with local judges who sometimes acted strangely indeed. Chief editors and solid lawyers can constitute an effective cabal.

After hair-raising test runs on the computer and a whole computer re-set over Sunday night after putting the last old Monday Globe to bed, we launched the redesigned Globe and Mail, with a new nameplate and all, on Tuesday, January 12, 1990, to broad approval. (Barbara Frum called that morning to say she rather liked it. She called again on Thursday to say she rather loved it.) Roy Megarry sent me a hand-written note that morning with congratulations, adding that he was looking forward to – expecting – even more conspicuous innovations in editorial content soon. We were in the daily newspaper business after all, so: "What have you done for me lately?" was quite appropriate. Roy was proud and maybe even a bit surprised. I was enormously thankful for the mandate he had given us with so much trust. He had made a considered bet, so far so good.

***

Three weeks later, I went to Paris for a few days, where the gay bars provided a remarkable array of beautiful young men. You must have humility in the face of beauty, and I did not lack humility.

I travelled on an overnight train to Venice, where I met friends Jeffrey Kofman and Michael Levine and visited the Biennale. Michael went off to study French while Jeff and I rented a car and travelled across northern Italy to Milan, then by train to Geneva, where my brother played an important role at the International Union for the Conservation of Nature (IUCN). In return, feeling secure in my job after the redesign, I sold my charming little house on Moore Avenue and bought a bigger, renovated house across the street backing onto Mount Pleasant Cemetery, where I lived for the next 20 years throwing many a memorable party. The ghosts haunting their graves just over the wall were pleased, I like to think: especially Glenn Gould.

I continued going to bars in Toronto's gay village, meeting the occasional treat. One night, a stranger came up and said, "What's it like to be the most powerful man in the bar?" I was 45 and replied that the most powerful man in the bar was the lithe twenty-something in great jeans leaning against the wall just over there. (I discovered later he was from Brazil and seeking asylum here.)

***

At some point, Roy came to my office to chat and got around to what he wanted to ask: Did I have any interest in someday becoming the publisher? I said I hoped he wasn't leaving. I said I loved the hands-on editing job and would like to put off any question like that for some years.

We had a retreat at the Millcroft Inn outside of Toronto in 1991 where Roy told me he was killing all the Globe magazines (Toronto, travel, fashion) except for ROB Magazine, which had been very profitable from the get-go in the mid-1980s. The new magazines (excellent in form and content) were losing a bundle with no real ad support. (The magazines were a separate department at The Globe, not reporting to me.)

Some months later, we had a post-mortem on the magazines at the Four Seasons in Toronto, including their departed staffs, chaired by Roy. It appeared these magazines had not gone through adequate comparative market analyses, and their staff had not been given detailed budgets and targets. The magazines were based on the success of Report on Business Magazine, the remit being something like, "Here is money, spend it well, and we will prosper." They spent it well, and we did not prosper. Roy cancelled the afternoon session, and the rest of us ate lunch alone together, looking out over the city from the top floor of the Four Seasons.

A few months later, Roy announced he would retire in the fall of 1992, after 14 years as publisher. That would introduce volatilities none of us could have foreseen and barely survived.

***

MEECH LAKE ACCORD: MULRONEY'S FATEFUL CALL

I was home on Saturday night, June 9, 1990, three days before our relaunch, when the telephone rang around 10:30 pm It was the prime minister, fresh from a dramatic week of meetings with the premiers trying to save the Meech Lake Accord. The Accord needed to be ratified by two remaining recalcitrant provinces (Manitoba and Newfoundland) by June 23 if it was to amend the Constitution Act of 1982 and win Quebec's signature to the document. The Globe had been fervent in support of the Accord, and I had watched the apparently successful outcome of that marathon session live on TV just minutes before.

Brian Mulroney was in high spirits and went into some detail about dynamics behind the scenes. I had a thought: The highly-publicized relaunch of The Globe and Mail would come three days later: Would the PM give us an exclusive interview about these historic meetings that we would place on the front page of that first, fresh Tuesday edition? I would send our top Ottawa journalists to conduct the interview on Monday (Jeff Simpson, Graham Fraser and Susan Delacourt). He agreed, asking that I not let anyone else know about it and to send our journalists to his official residence for privacy. I was delighted that we were fortuitously headed for a scoop about a critical national issue under our new nameplate on an auspicious day.

Monday in the newsroom was electric, as we made up pages with the new computer program, typography, layouts and features. We left a hole on the front page for the Mulroney interview. The copy came in around 5 pm, and I read it quickly, thinking it good in giving context to the political dynamics of Meech. In it went and appeared under a large picture of Newfoundland Premier Clyde Wells, apparently wavering already in his support of the Accord despite Saturday's agreement.

The dam burst Wednesday morning, as I was asked out of a management committee meeting to take a call from the PM. A storm of protest had arisen about his comment in the interview saying he had "rolled the dice" with the premiers the previous week, suggesting a form of manipulation and disrespect that had some of them boiling. I reread the piece and realized that this phrase might be provocative. Mr. Mulroney suggested he had been quoted out of context and sought clarification.

I went back to the editors, and we reviewed the text. I thought there might be a little room for clarification, but they adamantly disagreed. Meanwhile, stories flooded in about angry premiers and a threat to the Accord, as Mr. Mulroney argued he had been taken out of context. Opting for facts alone, I decided to run the text of the interview on the op-ed page the next day, and people could judge for themselves.

And judge they did. Liberal Opposition leader Sharon Carstairs rose in the Manitoba Legislature, holding the op-ed page in her hand, tore it in half and demanded that Manitoba reject the Accord. Premier Wells suspended his agreement of the previous weekend. The country was headed for a crisis of major proportions within two weeks.

The beleaguered PM called me from Newfoundland after addressing its legislature a few days later, saying he thought he had brought them around. (Speaking of Premier Clyde Wells a few weeks earlier, Mulroney said to me on the phone, "I don't know how to deal with a zealot. I've never dealt with Ayatollah Khomeini.") Votes in Newfoundland and Manitoba were set for June 23 itself – the deadline. Wells waited over several time zones to see what would happen in Manitoba, where Gary Filmon had a minority government that needed unanimous consent to bring the vote to the floor. A single indigenous member, Elijah Harper, raised a feather from a backbench opposing the motion, and the Accord was lost in Manitoba without a vote. Taking this cue, the slippery-sly Wells declined to bring it to a vote in Newfoundland, confirming the end. Plans for Mulroney and the premiers to walk triumphantly for Canada at the head of the St. Jean Baptiste national day parade in Montreal the following morning were cancelled.

Five years later, Canada would come within a whisker of losing the secession referendum in Quebec on account of this. And sooner, in the fall of 1991, Mr. Mulroney would have to stay put and reject the distinct possibility of becoming secretary-general of the United Nations, with the support of George H. W. Bush and other G7 leaders (China abstaining on the UN Security Council according to Mulroney). "I can't have you to dinner on the East River," he said to me, "but I'll buy you a steak and beer" in Canada sometime. Goodness.

How significant was the Mulroney interview in The Globe to the failure of the Meech Lake Accord two weeks later? The decisive move came from Elijah Harper, who was protesting the Accord from an indigenous point of view (though Canada's indigenous leaders all supported the Accord). It seems doubtful that the interview was material in Harper's judgment, though the accompanying storm, including Carstairs' performance in the Manitoba Legislature, may have emboldened him. Had Manitoba voted in favour, it seems likely that Newfoundland would have followed suit morosely. In all this, I felt very close to history, as I would in 1995 in the Quebec referendum, and then again through Mr. Mulroney's later travails over Airbus. We lived, as they say, in interesting times.

***

Bill Greenhalgh joined The Globe as our chief of operations, a talented and effective manager with a great sense of humour. We soon had a bond. Bill had a genius for seeing how operations could improve, bringing everyone along onside.

We all knew Roy was retiring during his last year onsite and wondered who the new person would be. One of our planning retreats featured the CEO of Campbell's Soup Canada, Dave Clark, who gave an evangelical-type speech over lunch about vision and change. Report on Business did a mildly mocking piece on him as an example of the new business gurus, radical agents of transformation. To us at lunch, he was a tangential showman.

One day in the summer of 1992, ROB editors came to me with a scoop: The new publisher of The Globe and Mail would be Dave Clark, from Campbell's Soup. I said I would try to confirm it, though they had good sources. I told Roy, who expressed disbelief. Thirty minutes later, he told me it was true, and I said we would run the story the next day. When it appeared, most everyone in Globe management was amazed. Dave Clark seemed on the face of it to be a very unlikely fit for The Globe.

Roy thought so, too, and went to Thomson Newspapers downtown to see what could be done. Clark was apparently bargaining with Campbell's in the U.S. for a big appointment there, holding off Thomson awhile in the process. However, he signed on as publisher, and there was nothing more Roy could do. We had a big country-themed farewell party for Roy downtown in the fall, with former Premier Bill Davis as Roy's "roaster." Then Roy, who had brought The Globe into the modern age as Canada's National Newspaper, and me in as editor-in-chief, was gone. Sort of.

It is important to think about how things would have been different without Roy Megarry as Publisher of The Globe and Mail. According to Roy, Conrad Black might have bought the paper in 1980 from FP, instead of the Thomsons, as Roy intervened on Thomson's side after meeting with Black at The Globe: Black would have upended the culture of that newspaper, not for the better.

Roy was prescient arguing for satellite transmission of The Globe across Canada several years later, at significant cost, knowing that "Canada's National Newspaper" needed to use this technology to meet its mandate. And Roy was much ahead of his time worrying about the "value-added" content journalism needed to invent to retain its readers in changing times.

Roy Megarry was a restless publisher in the best sense, looking over the hill and worried that a deeply conservative newsroom itself posed the greatest threat to the newspaper's sustainability. Newsrooms everywhere had elements of the Church, confident in their sense of right and mission. That was a danger I sensed and came to understand far better as editor-in-chief. Roy Megarry knew it from the start. It has metastasized thirty years later into overt media campaigns in news coverage to particular takes on social and environmental justice.

Then Roy made the radical decision to appoint William Thorsell as editor-in-chief of The Globe and Mail, not just after an afternoon with tea in his office but having known me for four years on the editorial board and as a writer in Report on Business Magazine. At the time, I wondered about that risky decision (for both of us). In retrospect, I think it was good. Eleven years later, in its content, The Globe was clearly ahead of its time, tightly bound to its readers and advertisers, and dominant at the core of Canadian journalism in a richer sense of that word. I would do some things differently now, of course, but it was a great run thanks to Roy Megarry. I do not think I let him down.

The following year was chaotic. Dave Clark brought along his long-time Campbell's Soup consultants from the United States, and Globe senior management spent many days at off-sites learning to be better people, revolutionary in outlook and behaviour. The consultants were exotic, leading us through all manner of exercises in hotel ballrooms to somehow improve our natures and marriages. It was torture.

Clark came from one of the lowest information-dense industries (food processing) to one of the highest (journalism) and was simultaneously intimidated and skeptical in his new environment (though he made efforts at outreach to us, which were appreciated). Meanwhile, a brutal recession had gripped Toronto in particular, and our financial metrics were collapsing. By spring 1993, we seemed to be heading for a loss on the year. Tensions ran high across all departments of the newspaper, and morale among senior management and the rest plummeted.

I could feel Clark's animosity grow toward me and to Bill Greenhalgh as we tried to keep a semblance of normality in our respective spheres. I learned from one of the rather distraught consultants that I was likely to be fired, and Bill was similarly at risk. Then came the climax.

Richard Harrington was the new CEO of Thomson Newspapers, based in Stamford, Conn. and ultimately responsible for The Globe. He would visit us personally, knowing how important The Globe was to Ken Thomson and his family. (Ken told me that the only thing that registered with his friends about his global assets was The Globe and Mail landing on their doorsteps every morning, and it mattered a great deal to him too.) It was apparent that Harrington was not impressed with Clark (whom he had not hired) and was losing patience with The Globe's financial travails. And Clark was feeling the pressure. I had appointed Margaret Wente as editor of the Daily Report of Business, and one day-end, Clark stopped by her office on his way home in evident distress. "Our balls are the line Peggy!" he said, to which she thought to herself, "Well, maybe yours."

Harrington came to Toronto with his team for a strategy summit at The Globe in the fall of 1993, attended by Ken Thomson, his sons David and Peter, and John Tory Sr., Ken's consigliere. Clark chaired the meeting in a claustrophobic boardroom and began to outline our strategy for recovery and growth.

At some point, Clark referred to a new Western edition of the paper to be produced out of Vancouver – a controversial idea opposed by Roy Megarry beyond the walls. Harrington started challenging Clark on the wisdom of such a move, becoming more aggressive by the minute. Suddenly, I was moved to say that the Western edition still had some analysis to be done, trying to give Clark some breathing space under Harrington's relentless battering. Harrington exploded in anger, asking if The Globe's management team knew what it was doing. He demanded that all of us from The Globe leave the room and that sandwiches be sent in for lunch. We were trembling as we headed down the hall, Harrington, the Thomsons, and their execs left alone to decide our fates.

Clark called us together in a fit of rage and confusion. He said there would be a special meeting of our management committee the next morning to deal with the fallout. Meanwhile, each of us had to prepare materials of various kinds. At some point, Clark's secretary called Bill Greenhalgh out of the meeting, and Bill returned fifteen minutes later, Clark still venting fury. We were under dark clouds indeed.

Bill came to my office and said he had been called out for a phone call. It was Richard Harrington on the company plane heading back to Stamford. He wanted Bill and me to know that he had full confidence in us and that Clark would not be long for The Globe. Bill and I were floored and, of course, thrilled. Clark called each of us individually into his office soon after to say he was leaving. To me, he said he and his consultants were willing to help me, nevertheless going forward, to overcome my "biases" in editing the paper. I nodded thanks and never saw him again.

I never blamed Dave Clark for being hired as Publisher at The Globe, a decision taken by the then-president of Thomson Newspapers who himself departed soon after. It was a lesson in the importance of the hiring decision, the importance of matching not just skills but sensibilities to the agenda for change. (There is always an agenda for change in hiring a CEO.) We had just experienced a profound and foreseeable mismatch among such things at The Globe, paid a high price for the year (as did Clark), and came close to losing critical human assets along the way.

In how many organizations does this happen with worse consequences? Too many, if we read the business pages. Professional headhunters charge a lot for a successful hire, and they deserve the fee if it works. The stakes are often higher than they appear, for better and for worse.

***

SOME GAY LIFE

I was driving home up Yonge Street on a lovely spring day and stopped at a light north of Bloor. Walking on the sidewalk was Philip, the guy I had met perhaps six years before and had missed much after our separation. I called him through the window, and he got in. We went to my place nearby for a drink, and I found that he had been teaching English in South Korea and was back now to find a permanent job.

We started hanging out again, and this time I learned that he had a bipolar condition, which explained much of his odd behaviour in retrospect. He attributed it to diet and spent many hours in the Toronto Reference Library reading up on food intolerances, ranging from peanut butter to eggs. I did some reading of my own, and suggested he look at medications, which he rejected as crutches that indicated weakness. Then Prozac came along, which appeared to be much better than lithium and such generally in play. I made a parallel to diabetes, saying that taking insulin to offset your body's lack of the same was no sign of weakness, rather of intelligence. He finally agreed to try Prozac.

It made a huge initial difference. Suddenly, he could concentrate enough to do what he loved most – read. And we could have long discussions about the contents of The Economist, to which I gave him a subscription. We were always conversing and joking and enjoying each other's company in the night. He got a job at a call centre, and we kept on, kibitzing about maybe someday sharing a house.

His swings between manic and depressive states began to recur and intensify. Ultimately, it became clear that a stable relationship was going to be difficult (perhaps more clear to me). I didn't believe I had the internal resources to cope with the distressing amplitudes he experienced, to my great sadness. We committed to a simple friendship, and I saw less of him.

A year later, he appeared in my garden one spring day to say he had been diagnosed as HIV-positive. We both had a good cry. I got tested and came through negative. The "cocktail" was thankfully present just then, and he started on it. We went to some movies, and one day, I drove him to the land I had bought in the country north of the city. He was obviously ill, and we said we'd call. We didn't. (I didn't.) Two years later, his brother phoned to say he had died of cancer at 37.

Philip was the one guy I met in Toronto after I arrived in 1984 with whom I considered sharing a life. He was intelligent, passionate about politics and society, warm and handsome. I will always wonder if I had had more strength and imagination, it could have been. Maybe I was simply selfish – a reasonable hypothesis.

I lost lovers, friends and acquaintances to AIDs over some 15 years and feared for more. I wrote music for piano in four sections to help deal with this in the 1990s. I still play it every few days.

Over those decades in the city, I hoped to find a partner in life and tracked a few candidates. But, with the exception of Philip, I never found reciprocation and sometimes wondered if my heart was really into coupling after all. I valued my privacy and autonomy in the context of a vibrant social existence. But I do think, save for his burden of bipolar and my faint of heart, Philip and I could have made a credible stab at life together. It was not to be.

***

I linked up with my friend Max from Princeton, who was now living with his partner Joe in Washington, D.C., where Max worked at the World Bank. Every other week, Joe's two young children lived at their home, reverting to their mother's house alternately. I visited them, and we got along well. Max grew up in Peru to a French mother and Swiss father, and we started to share holidays in

Paris, where Max had cousins. The three of us rented an apartment for two weeks each summer and settled into life on the streets and galleries and shops. It was a wonderful tradition. Max and Joe came to Toronto to explore the gay city and spend weekends at my country place. Around 2008, Max encountered cancer and died a year later. Joe and I have maintained our friendship since.

***

MULRONEY ON THE PHONE

Prime Minister Brian Mulroney took to calling me frequently – the most fateful one in June 1990, where he agreed to the interview that contributed to the collapse of the Meech Lake Accord. He became comfortable chatting on background about all manner of things, rarely amounting to a news story, but always providing context and insight into his points of view. My assistant, Heather Macleod, would seek me out of newsroom meetings, stroking her chin to indicate the PM was on the line. Everybody got the message, and there was a combination of understanding and disapproval at my frequent contact with the prime minister. (Our national columnist, Jeffrey Simpson, refused to accept calls from Mulroney, believing them inherently compromising. Journalism lacks a consensus on this.)

With one exception (described later), I never placed a call to the PM, and I never pretended to give advice, which would have been inconsistent with my role. (I did that only on the pages of The Globe and Mail.) My aim was to hear him out, to learn as much as I could about the subject at hand, taking notes along the way. I missed the hint one afternoon in 1993 when he called and tried to convey he would announce his retirement the next day.

Otherwise, it was off-record background and context, often filled with spicy descriptions of his opponents and colleagues and consistently flattering to himself. (Pierre Trudeau "says I was servile to the Americans. I think that's fair comment coming from a man who was closer to Fidel Castro.")

Most interesting were his calls about conversations with leaders of the G7, Russia, or members of the Commonwealth and Francophonie. Brian Mulroney is a classic extrovert and networker, who found himself prime minister of a middling country that was a member of virtually every significant club in the world. He revelled in the access he had to the White House and the Kremlin, to Berlin and London and Paris.

And he developed close personal ties with most of the leaders of these countries over time. (Francois Mitterrand said to him, "I love the Germans so much, I think we should have two of them." Michael Gorbachev called Mulroney Aug. 22, 1991, after the aborted coup against him in Russia: "They tried to break my spine.... Thank God the bodyguards were on my side.") He became their confidant and frequently the bridge between and among them – a fixer on a world stage that arose directly from his own personality and capacity, perfectly aligned with Canada's connections to everything that mattered.

(External Affairs Minister Joe Clark, who lost the Tory leadership to Mulroney in 1983, spent most of his time outside the country staying clear of Mulroney's files – an elegant arrangement that suited them both. Clark said to me at lunch in Edmonton after Mulroney beat him at the 1983 convention, "The best man lost." I rarely met a man whose pride was more impregnable than that of Joe Clark, agreeing on this with Mulroney, who rarely separated the words "Joe Clark" from "vanity." Referring to Clark's role in the 1993 convention that chose Kim Campbell as PC leader with Clark's help, Mulroney said to me: "Our friend Mr. Clark, I tell you, this guy has a lemming-like instinct unparalleled in Canadian history.")

Ronald Reagan and George H. W. Bush, in particular, came to rely on Mr. Mulroney for counsel in dealing with matters domestic and international. Mulroney spent Bush's last weekend in the office with him at Camp David in January 1992, having foreseen Bush's defeat in the election. Mulroney gave eulogies at both Ronald Reagan's and George Bush's funerals, and both US presidents were much weaker individually than you might think: Mulroney knew them and backed them up off-line. He placed me beside George H. W. Bush at a dinner in Montreal in 1997, and the gap between their capacities was obvious.

Mulroney played a role in bridging views among the G7 and Russia about German reunification, earning a specific credit from Chancellor Helmut Kohl after the deed was done. He heard out an inebriated Boris Yeltsin on the phone for more than an hour one Christmas eve when Yeltsin wanted company. Mulroney could see the gaps in people's capacities and relationships, and knew how to fill them. You don't learn this kind of thing in school, rather perhaps in the school of life.

Canada has never been more influential in international relations than it was during Mulroney's time, and much of it was ad hominem. The platform of Canada-in-the-world was a perfect fit for the kid from Baie Comeau. Canada gave Brian Mulroney a favoured seat in global affairs, and he exercised that Canadian opportunity brilliantly, including on human rights and the environment.

(In this, he was assisted in Washington by our ambassador, Allan Gotlieb, whom Mulroney did not dismiss in 1984 when he assumed office. However, that did not stop Mulroney from objecting strongly to

Gotlieb's "suckhole piece" in The Globe and Mail, Jan. 4, 1994, in which Gotlieb wrote of then-Prime Minister Jean Chretien's superior opportunities in Canada's relations with Washington. "Its thrust was at complete variance with the opinions you expressed to me over the years you served as our Ambassador in Washington," Mulroney wrote to Gotlieb that week. The letter, of which I received a copy, was an angry rebuke to Gotlieb's provocative suggestion that Chretien would be more effective than Mulroney in defence of Canada's interests.)

Mr. Mulroney's domestic record was considerably more patchy. Significant achievements on North American free trade, deregulation, the environment and tax reform were offset by two overhanging emergencies in national unity and national debt/deficits when he resigned in 1993. Then there was the later trauma of Karlheinz Schreiber in the Airbus Affair. The emergencies passed, as did the trauma. What endured were substantial achievements, to his good fortune, though the whole of the record will never go away.

The leadership race to succeed Mulroney in 1993 became somewhat bizarre. Kim Campbell was the much-touted successor – an ideal demographic: female, British Columbian, apparently smart and allegedly multilingual

(including Russian). It was her great lead that convinc
most of the other likely candidates to skip the rac
Barbara McDougall, Michael Wilson, Perrin Beatty. It was
starting to look like a cakewalk.

Mr. Mulroney called to say he was deeply concerned
about this. The party needed a race to generate publicity,
but more importantly, it needed a race because the PM
was not at all sure that Kim Campbell had the stuff to do
the job. (He had been very critical to me for her
performance as Minister of Justice – she couldn't get the
caucus onside for enhancements to human rights
legislation.) She had to be tested through a real
leadership race, and there needed to be a backup if she
fell apart. But the field was quickly narrowing.

Mr. Mulroney called one afternoon to say he had
heard Jean Charest was planning a news conference to
announce that he, too, would stay out of the race.
Mulroney said he had asked Charest to come to 24 Sussex
that evening for a heart-to-heart: Charest had a profound
duty to run, he argued rather forcefully: "You can be a
has-been, a might have been or the leader. If you don't
run, you'll be one of the first two." The next morning,
Mulroney called to say Charest was on his way to
Toronto to announce his candidacy.

Mr. Mulroney continued his calls to me well into the 2000s, sharing stories and opinions and, later, even testing speeches, text and eulogies. Beyond self-interest, he came to confide in me, and I valued the conversations, as he must have done as well. Years ago, senior journalists were expected to have trusted relationships with leading public figures, such as Peter Lougheed, Senator Keith Davey and Brian Mulroney, so to better understand events. In my time, many journalists regarded such links as compromising in essence. I knew that and opted, in any case, to learn more by allowing myself to know leading players in many fields somewhat, secure in my sense of proper distances. I believe I was a better journalist in consequence, and again, there is no consensus on that.

(I went only once to the PM's official residence at 24 Sussex Drive for dinner in honour of Javier Perez de Cuellar, who, on stepping down as secretary-general of the United Nations, gave all the gifts he had received in office to the Canadian Museum of Civilization. At our table, I asked why a diplomat from Peru had chosen this museum to bequeath his collection. He said, "I have travelled everywhere in the world in my capacities as a diplomat. And I have concluded that Canada is the country the world needs to learn to become." It was

Canada's capacity to meld diverse cultures into a functional whole over centuries that moved him. It moved me too.)

***

DAVOS MAN

Lunch on the magic mountain

I attended the World Economic Forum in Davos for ten years as a member of their "Media Leaders Club" and latterly a member of the WEF program committee. Davos provided an annual dip into exalted worlds of political and economic power, intellectual currents and technological developments. The days were filled with seminars, speeches and coffee klatches. The evenings were intimate dinners and lavish parties. I emerged from ten days there with a better appreciation of international trends, technological change and personalities, appreciating the flashy celebrity of it all.

Peter and Melanie Munk hosted Canadians attending Davos to dinner each year at their place in Klosters, twenty minutes down the mountainside. Here, with a few international stars, we settled into the conspicuous consumption of goods, services and status, to be sure. (Laurent Beaudoin explained to me in detail over dinner his plans for an extended-range business jet at Bombardier.)

I caught a ride back to Davos in the limo of Scotiabank CEO Peter Godsoe one night, sharing the car with George Soros. We got talking about Europe after the fall of the USSR, and I intoned that we would need to relearn the skills of balance-of-power politics in a newly multipolar world, and that would include respecting Russia's immediate sphere of influence in Eastern Europe. Soros responded fiercely that this was no time for the faint-of-heart in dealing with Russia, and we needed to seize our opportunities to instil liberal democratic values in that region especially. I deferred, and he glared as we arrived in snowy Davos, history to be continued. (Two years later, at a Bilderberg meeting in Finland with Conrad Black, I kicked myself for failing to challenge the consensus that the EU and NATO should expand right up to Russia's borders: Is there no understanding of existential space?)

At a media-club breakfast in the mid-1990s, I asked Bill Gates what, beyond shopping, he thought the most important consequence would be of the emerging internet. He said, "Give me a minute to think." Then, framed by a large window before a snow-covered forest patrolled by Swiss army guys with Airedales, he said "email." Email would vastly accelerate the process of discovery as millions of like minds concentrated on solving equations and all manner of human puzzles. None of us "intellectuals" took the next step to imagine Facebook and kin, but Gates remained a billionaire anyway. And none of us imagined the downside of trolls, espionage, crime, rampant narcissism and such. Or the death of many newspapers, not just due to ad revenue declines, but their role as gatekeepers for information. I would come to say, "The printing press allowed one to speak to many; the telephone allowed one to speak to one; the internet allowed many to speak to many."

Davos allowed global leaders of every stripe to mingle informally and discreetly in a "safe space" where options could be explored and deals done. Sitting beside Bob Rae in the audience, to see Shimon Peres lead Yasser Arafat by the hand onto the stage for a discussion about peace in Israel was something special. To see Hillary Clinton give a strong, unscripted speech about the strength of civil society one week after the Lewinsky revelations was impressive indeed.

I chaired a panel one year on the Uses and Misuses of History with Desmond Tutu, Timothy Garten Ash and Daniel Boorstin. I asked them to address the question: "What makes history a Balm - or a Burden?" Tutu replied that truth and reconciliation provided the balm (he was chair of the commission in South Africa). Garten Ash said a bit about a lot. It was Boorstin, then Librarian of the U.S. Congress, who shocked the audience in arguing that history is often so toxic it should be ignored so as not to infect the current culture. That roiled many questions: "– What forget the Holocaust!" - and made for a memorable panel in Davos lore.

(Teaching history at the University of Alberta in the 1970s, I intoned, "We study history to get rid of it," drawing a parallel to amnesiacs who need to learn about their past to leave it behind and engage robustly with the future. I realized later, on the contrary, that history often sticks far too much with us, thus my question to the Davos panellists. I think both Tutu and Boorstin were right, and the matter is situational and applies to individual psychology as well. Currently, I favour Boorstin's admonition.)

Flying overnight once from Toronto to Zurich on the way to Davos, I was invited to the cockpit to see how Air Canada's Airbus worked. Under a full moon over the Atlantic, the computer altered the heading slightly as our designated runway changed three hours out. On one return leg from Zurich, the pilot invited Sonja Bata up to witness the landing at Toronto's Pearson Airport. We cheered her on, though it was a rather rough landing.

I thought of working at the World Economic Forum just as the ROM came along in 2000, despite the Forum's reputation as a volatile work environment. It would have been an adventure at a time before "Davos Man" became a derisory term for "globalists" who did not comprehend the alienation and regression that millions of people were experiencing around the world. The Great Recession of 2008 torqued that critique, and Davos now struggles to "recalculate."

***

Launching colour with Roger Parkinson, 1998. Photo
credit Ed Lum

With Dave Clark gone as the publisher, we revived
with enthusiasm at The Globe and Mail. Bill Greenhalgh
emerged as our spark and leader, with a tight focus on
practical issues and team rebuilding. We had an offsite at
the Admiral Hotel on Toronto's waterfront for some 40
senior managers from all departments to set out the

agenda. Naturally, there was much speculation about who the new publisher might be. Suddenly, a group rose from the floor and made a motion that we support Bill Greenhalgh as publisher. The motion passed with great enthusiasm, including my own, but how to communicate this to Thomson Corp.? The room deputized me to do so.

I called Dick Harrington in Stamford and reported the events and my support for the motion. He was polite and non-committal. We knew then that he had asked Roy Megarry to return as an interim publisher, and we also knew that neither Bill nor I were in Roy's good books now. (Responding to a call from Harrington, Bill Greenhalgh said he preferred an operating role elsewhere in Thomson to a contested process to be the publisher of The Globe.)

And so it was some months later in 1994 that we met our new boss, Roger Parkinson, a fifties-something retired newspaper publisher from Minneapolis, Minn., who had no knowledge of Canada or The Globe. In his manner, on the other hand, he was very much in the image of Roy Megarry, suave and tailored.

Bill Greenhalgh soon left The Globe, having effectively served as publisher for more than six months and now pre-empted. Bill was a significant loss – a fine manager, strong leader, filled with ideas and tech-savvy. We would miss him. I wondered what was next.

Roger was nice around me, tentative. I was polite and properly responsive but not ingratiating. We carried on warily for a while when Roger burst into my office late one afternoon to say he had just heard I had lied about my availability for an upcoming meeting and that lying to him was a firing offence. I had no idea what Roger was talking about. I said my secretary, who had left for the day, could substantiate this the next morning, which she did. I asked Roger for an apology, which he delivered. The episode had all the makings of a trivial excuse for what was yet to come – my dismissal. I started pondering my options yet again.

The weeks ticked on, and news about our business kept improving: Ontario was emerging from its terrible early-90s recession. Roger had an intellectual bent and a love for public policy. We had the best editorial board in the history of The Globe and Mail, and Roger called one morning to say he thought our editorials were superb, and that morning in particular. (My editorial board: Marcus Gee, Andrew Cohen, Andrew Coyne, Tony Keller – a diversity of white men.) The board met every morning at 11, each member to propose a topic and analysis within his fields of expertise. Our discussions were vibrant and often led to altered viewpoints after the initial play. Andrew Coyne frequently changed our minds about economics. Andrew Cohen was a literary master about all things Canadian and American. Tony Keller – the neophyte – found his feet over time across the horizon. And Marcus Gee dominated international affairs. I wrote maybe one editorial a week myself, usually in relation to constitutional issues, where we found it difficult to reach a consensus. Ultimately, if necessary, the editor-in-chief constituted a majority of one (risky for me to go on holidays).

One morning around 1995, Marcus Gee proposed that we support gay marriage as an extension of our consistent commitment to human rights. I asked for opinions, and there was quick agreement, though no one thought this was imminent. I made no comment on the issue. When Marcus's editorial appeared the next morning, it caused quite a stir, and many believed it had come from me. It did not. On gay issues, I left the initiatives to the board.

Meanwhile, Roger Parkinson and I visited the bureaus in Ottawa and Montreal, where Brian Mulroney held a cocktail party at his home in Westmount to welcome Roger to Canada and made favourable comments about The Globe. On our way to the airport home, Roger was ebullient.

After this tentative start, Roger Parkinson became an effective and supportive publisher, growing in trust of me and the newsroom. He supported my case to delay the use of colour in the news pages through new off-set presses in Toronto that we had contracted to an outside supplier. The use of colour in the news space would add $2-million annually to our production costs. If those funds were available, I argued we invest them instead in a major content upgrade to Report on Business and some other sections. ROB was facing serious competition from the daily Financial Post after some years of disinvestment under Dave Clark, in particular. Roger bravely agreed to this. On a certain Friday, six of the Post's major assets walked into their editor's office and said they were leaving for The Globe and Mail – including Andrew Willis and Paul Waldie. With added space and talent, the ROB vaulted back to the top, which was critical to our fortunes.

The new presses gave us superb reproduction in colour for Toronto advertisers and also in black, white and greys for editorial content. I put a team together under art director Michael Gregg, including Stuart Ash again from the outside, to strengthen our 1990 redesign, which had lost some of its discipline and force. Hewing closely to the original vision, we strengthened body-types, graphics and layouts, and re-launched the black and white and "grey" Globe and Mail to some fanfare. It was beautiful and effective, and we entered The Globe's refreshed design in the Financial Post's annual competition for design and branding, which was judged by an independent jury. We won the top prize just ahead of TD Bank's green logo and easy chair. The Financial Post honourably ran a memorable photo of our design team in their coverage about our win.

Our Saturday edition had always been the poor cousin of the daily, lacking ad support from ROB or Special Reports, relying instead on low line-rate retail and entertainment ads, and was somewhat thin in content. Its circulation hovered around 300,000, compared with 318,000 for the week-daily. Saturday's edition was the only one of the week that lost money, and some management committee members dumbly nagged to have it killed. This is where Roger Parkinson shone.

(We looked at this when Roy Megarry was publisher, and he authorized us to probe the possibility of a Sunday Globe and Mail. We thought it might consist of a high-quality Sunday Globe magazine, and I had a prototype made upon beautiful paper sourced in northern Ontario. We took it to focus groups who loved it but insisted it be wrapped in Saturday's sports scores and the latest news. Without discussion, Roy said the project was dead and instructed me to destroy every prototype of the Sunday Globe magazine (like the Avro Arrow). Which I did, except for a box of those lovely dream magazines still in my basement.

I proposed to invest quite heavily in the Saturday edition – to be known as The Weekend Edition – with special attention to the arts, books, Focus (public policy; science) and personal finance in ROB. We proposed that readers pay for this expanded edition through a much higher cover price. We would go from 50 cents a copy to $1 over the first year, then higher after establishing the value proposition for readers through much better content.

There were few precedents for such a strategy, and I made a bet with Paul Steiger, my equivalent at The Wall Street Journal, that we could pull it off. With strong support from Dmitri Chrus, our savvy director of circulation, and after much hee-hawing, Roger agreed to support this gambit. "The Weekend Starts Here," said our vigorous ad campaign, and we launched to great fanfare at 50 cents.

Within a year or so, the Weekend Edition was reaching 400,000 circulations, and we were charging a full dollar a copy – enough to make money on single-copy sales alone. It also justified an increase in subscription rates. This was something of the Holy Grail for journalism then (and now): shifting the burden of revenue from advertisers to readers based on conspicuously higher value to readers. Ad revenue rose in tandem.

By 1997, weekly circulation revenue for all editions was up 79 percent, and circulation costs were flat (compared with 1991). Circulation profit was up 419 percent, and the newsroom budget as a percentage of circulation revenue fell from 90 percent in 1991 to 67 percent. We estimated that our Ideal Circulation strategy of 1991 and content changes were contributing $23.9-million annually to the bottom line.

Mike Brophy arrived as our new head of HR. "I know what you're thinking," he said at our first meeting: "Watch out, here comes help." But help he was, both in establishing a proper annual bonus program for senior management and in coaching me on how to better bring the newsroom around to my vision for the paper. I first did "listening sessions" with every person in the newsroom in groups of 15 or so. (I conspicuously took notes at each session and tried to find at least one immediate action response from each one.) Then I followed with "strategy sessions" describing The Globe's place in the industry and my vision for high-utility journalism that went well beyond "what went wrong yesterday." (It centred on a news "quadrant" divided between past and future, problems, solutions, dangers and opportunities.) I learned to be a better manager and leader through all this. Morale began to recover and even shine based on our surveys, rising from the depths after Clark's tenure. We started making valuable long-term agreements with our unions.

Our strategies to strengthen The Globe and Mail's distinctive journalism, relationship to its readers and advertisers, marketing and production efficiencies were clearly paying off by all our metrics. (This included dominance at the National Newspaper Awards in most categories, notably commentary and investigative reporting in ROB.) The Canadian economy was reviving after five terrible years, and our profits were rising nicely. Roger was expressing full confidence now in the editorial team, enjoying his publisher role. We hosted a lavish Globe and Mail 150th birthday bash in a hangar on the Toronto Islands. What could possibly go wrong?

***

PM KIM CAMPBELL

PM Campbell after the Editorial Board, 1993, Photo
Credit Ed Lum

The contest to replace Brian Mulroney as leader of
the Progressive Conservative Party came down to Kim
Campbell and Jean Charest in the spring of 1993.
Campbell was the incipient winner by almost every

calculation, but in my calls from Mulroney, I kept hearing his doubts about Campbell's capacities. "She has the possibility of a historic calamity on her hands," he said in April, two months before the convention, "It has to do with leadership... She doesn't have the quality of leadership."

It reduced, it appeared, to her powers of concentration, strategic sensibilities and lack of human touch, all of which Mulroney feared for. In due course, Campbell and Charest came in individually to meet The Globe's editorial board. The results seemed obvious to us: Campbell was flying by the seat of her pants, while Charest had a head on his shoulders and feet on the ground. We endorsed Charest for PC leader.

As we got into May, Mulroney's calls to me became more frequent and agitated, to the point that he revealed he was doing what he could within the imminent convention to see Charest prevail. He criticized Campbell's "tone-deafness" and apparently scattered approach to issues and people. "Somebody's got quite a trivial idea of what the real issues are." By the convention's opening in early June, Mulroney was fully committed to Charest, believing Campbell posed a serious threat to the party's future.

In the event, Campbell's big lead within the PCs evaporated, and she came within a whisker of losing that convention to Charest. Mulroney's work behind the scenes came close to changing the outcome, but a whisker was all she needed. Kim Campbell would be prime minister by the end of June.

The weeks of transition were, in Mulroney's frequent calls, almost entirely discouraging. One day after her victory at the convention, "Campbell wanted Charest out." He said Campbell failed to reach out to Charest or his supporters, was alienating her cabinet colleagues with indifference and blew off his suggestions about stating her priorities and vision when she officially assumed office. (He had provided her with thorough briefing books.) "We're off to a bad start." She was winging it on every level, from his point of view to the point he called her in to remonstrate, to no avail, saying at one point, "I'm still PM and the way you're acting, I'm having second thoughts about turning it over to you." In Mulroney's view, Campbell believed "she's a cross between Madonna and Mother Teresa."

As Campbell became prime minister at the end of June, Mulroney was filled with foreboding about the future of the regime, though he said to Campbell, "If you win 250 seats, I'll send you the design for my statue." And off he went to France with his family for a holiday at the summer house of President Francois Mitterrand, among his more appreciative friends. He said he would miss three things, especially after leaving office: the Wednesday meeting of caucus, the power of appointment, and Harrington Lake.

Campbell was standing near 50 percent in public opinion polls when she called the general election in September and started falling immediately as she stated in front of Rideau Hall that elections were not the time to discuss serious issues, such as unemployment. She visited our editorial board the day her economic platform was released, facing the likes of Andrew Coyne, Marcus Gee, Margaret Wente, Terry Corcoran, Tony Keller and myself. She was alone except for one public affairs aide and had just flown in overnight from Vancouver. It was soon apparent that she had either not fully read the platform or did not understand the central parts of it. After a time, we were reduced to an embarrassed silence as she flailed and grappled away. I walked her out of the building, smiling broadly with a sense of chagrin for us all.

Of course, we could not endorse her in the election, and Jean Chretien's Liberals swept to power, leaving the

PCs with three seats in Parliament (not including Campbell's). The caucus "will know what to do," said Mulroney, if she didn't resign immediately. Deputy Prime Minister Donald Mazankowski said, "We let a stranger take over the party." Mulroney was "horrified by her campaign, horrified by her political stupidity. I thought she was going to win, and then she opened her mouth."

A lot of people blamed that outcome on Mulroney, but he weighed in against her during the PC leadership campaign, Prime Minister Campbell launched her federal election campaign at 50 percent in opinion polls, and she rode down the hill pretty much on her own, as Mulroney feared she would. (John Tory, later a hapless leader of Ontario's Tories and then a good mayor of Toronto, was her campaign manager.)

***

GLOBE AND MAIL: REGIME CHANGE

Stuart Garner arrived in Toronto from Britain in 1995 to become President of Thomson Newspapers, a division of Thomson Corp. The days were gone when publisher Roy Megarry essentially bypassed Thomson Newspapers and dealt directly with Ken Thomson and John Tory Sr. downtown. The Globe's publisher now reported to the President of Thomson Newspapers, and that was now Stuart Garner. Garner came from a mid-market, middle-brow British newspaper background and disliked The Globe and Mail, which he found dense, eccentric, overly concentrated on politics, business and the arts, unforgivably light on sport and greatly lacking in "human interest" stories.

His attitude made complete sense to me, given his provenance and the nature of even "quality" papers in the UK. (In this context, someone in his orbit advised me to put a big picture frequently on The Globe's front page of a woman with ample breasts or a cute animal. Better: display such a woman holding a puppy.) I had become a snob.

Soon after arriving in Toronto, Garner asked what my favourite newspapers were, and I answered the New

York Times, The Wall Street Journal (where we shared a news-sharing partnership) and the Financial Times of London. "All boring," he said, and I knew we were in for interesting times.

Our publisher, the refined Roger Parkinson, bore the brunt of Garner's drumbeat of contempt for The Globe, despite our robust reader and advertiser numbers and rising profitability. Roger started warning me of trouble ahead.

In 1998, we were introduced to a new general manager of The Globe, Phillip Crawley, another mid-market Brit who had worked in Hong Kong and then in New Zealand. Garner brought Crawley to Toronto as his man in The Globe, purportedly reporting to Parkinson. Consultants arrived in the newsroom with ideas to "spark up" our presentation. Maybe we could write more lively leads. We could all feel the control of The Globe slipping away.

Meanwhile, Conrad Black announced he was starting a competing national newspaper against the very profitable Globe, after reportedly failing to convince Ken Thomson to sell him The Globe instead. Black apparently said The Globe would never be worth more than the day of his offer if Black went up against it. (Conrad had failed to buy The Globe from FP in 1980 in competition with Thomson: Black was a jilted suitor and went on to much more arresting travails.)

That torqued Garner's team enormously, and accelerated our introduction of colour to the news pages on July 9, 1998. We explored various strategies to counter Black's challenge, and decided to double down on our core missions of national, international and business news, with some added emphasis on "human interest" and sport. Research confirmed our readers ' identification with The Globe and expressed fears of "dumbing down" in response to new competition. We analyzed Black's business case for his new paper and could find nothing but large future losses for him and his shareholders. How could they approve that? What was he up to? Had we missed something?

The National Post appeared in October 1998, and was impressive in many ways, with an enormous budget for staff and newsprint under a gifted editor in Ken Whyte (whom I had hired some years earlier as Alberta columnist for The Globe). We did comparative analyses each morning and concluded over time that the Post would not prevail over our core missions, including commentary, where the Post was far to the right and unaccountably focused on supporting Israel. There was intense competition in the circulation departments, of course, but our surveys of readers and advertisers showed high degrees of loyalty as the months passed.

Not to mention that we had a determined Ken Thomson with us, prepared to spend whatever more might be necessary to win the day – much more than Mr. Black could muster. (Ken pestered me on this, probing whether we were spending enough money in the face of the Post.) Black sold the money-losing Post to CanWest in 2000-2001. Major cuts in the Post's budget saw the departure of editor Ken Whyte in 2003. The war was over.

Nevertheless, we came to work one day in 1999 to find that Phillip Crawley would now serve as publisher, Roger Parkinson elevated to "Chairman."

A few weeks later, Crawley informed me that he would seek an editor for the paper (from the UK), who would serve under me as editor-in-chief. He assured me in April that my position was secure in light of these changes, though it would obviously evolve. (Crawley had earlier ordered me to fire Margaret Wente as managing editor, a provocation to be sure. I convinced him that we should keep her at The Globe as a columnist, where she bloomed for decades to come.)

I had decided in January 1999, after ten years as editor-in-chief (and a birthday cake in the newsroom), that I would resign effective January 1, 2000, and return to writing, a scenario that Roy Megarry and I had agreed upon years before. I planned to inform Crawley of this at Canadian Thanksgiving in October.

In June, I gave a major presentation to the World Association of Newspapers in Zurich, Switzerland, on how The Globe had responded to the creation of the National Post. In early July, Crawley informed me that he was terminating my employment at The Globe entirely one year later on my 55th birthday. Meanwhile, I would serve as chair of the editorial board and continue my weekly column. This was no surprise to me, and I immediately offered full cooperation to my successor – and started severance negotiations.

I settled in for the duration, writing and editing and, after some emotional turbulence (shared generously by Rosie and Itchie Abella), feeling quite serene about my 16 years at The Globe and Mail, confident in my contributions there and beyond. Journalism was a tribe, hewing to a certain range of core concepts, and I was intent on widening the field. That worked well with our readers in my time, then reverted to form from within.

The "gay Norwegian from Alberta" was gone. Stuff happens.

I had been prepared for this moment as the "winds of change" blew all more fiercely through Thomson Newspapers and The Globe. A few years earlier, Thomson called its executives together in Florida from almost two hundred newspapers in North America to say Thomson was abandoning print publication and that every title except The Globe and Mail would be sold. (Ken would keep The Globe as a family heirloom.) Going forward, Thomson Corp. would operate on three principles in selling information: Its markets would be global; its content would be proprietary, meaning specific to Thomson, such as legal or financial data; and Thomson would distribute only by digital means to eliminate circulation costs. Conventional newspapers were doomed, and Thomson had a brilliant strategy to exit. And so they did – and so it was - brilliant.

(At a Q&A at that meeting, I asked Ken Thomson from the floor why Thomson did not provide us with an opportunity to earn discounted company shares as part of our compensation. He replied that company shares fluctuated, and it would be unfair to his employees to have them share the risk. Murmurs rippled through the crowd.)

At The Globe and Mail, I had determined I would do nothing to damage my own situation or that of the paper when the moment came – I had put far too much into my career to see it compromised by these events. One week later, Phillip appeared in my office with Ken and David Thomson, who had not been consulted on the matter, as Roger Parkinson had not. They expressed much appreciation for my decade at the helm, and Ken said I was secure in my employment at The Globe for as long as I wished into the future, catching Phillip off guard. Ken and David were entirely gracious.

Might I have stayed on indefinitely as Roy and I had foreseen, and Ken would have allowed, to write? Maybe, but it went against my instincts. First, I had been editor-in-chief for almost eleven years: Former CEOs should not hang around the plant. Second, I was 54, and had been in newspaper journalism for almost 25 years: Having bounced around so much in my youth, was I now to default to more-of-the-same at that still-prescient age? Third, I had seen people in many fields grow into gargoyles, carrying on beyond some cosmic due date, even as they waved their fading flags. They became clichés of themselves, a kind of papier-mache obstruction in the ebullient flow of life. I couldn't abide it.

In retrospect as well, it was a good time to leave the industry. The internet had not yet gutted newspaper revenues or created the alternate news feeds that draw so many readers elsewhere. My successors had to deal with deepening troughs of scarcity. Many of my colleagues referred to the 1990s as a golden age, the last hurrah of a doomed paradigm. In subsequent years, readers stopped me on Toronto streets expressing nostalgia for the once "fat" and quirky Globe. That Globe was no longer possible.

I would not have had the skills or inclination to thrive in these new circumstances, I think, much less recent ones where identity politics have so corroded the intellectual and ethical norms we once held in high regard. (Martin Luther King hoped to be judged someday by the content of his character, rather than the colour of his skin: not yet; not now.) Too, we aspired to some vision of "objectivity" in covering events, now conspicuously rejected, as we see in the vibrant dedication of newspapers and broadcasters to social missions. What does a classic liberal do in these circumstances? Newsrooms pose the greatest challenge to their own legitimacy now, and newsrooms do not like mirrors.

That said, Canada is blessed that its national newspaper is privately owned by the Thomson family, who understand its role and have provided essential ballast for more than 40 years. The paper has managed through revolutionary times well and remains pre-eminent in Canada's public life. The legacy endures.

The question for me was, "What's next?"

***

AIRBUS WITH A VENGEANCE

The fall of 1995 was a critical time for Canada and, as it turned out, for Brian Mulroney. Quebec's second referendum on separation from Canada was set for October 30, after the failure of the Meech Lake Accord in 1990, and the Charlottetown Accord in 1992, both on Mulroney's watch. In September 1995, Mr. Mulroney (now working as a lawyer in Montreal) started calling me to warn that the contest was much closer than most people believed: The polls were underestimating the risk, and Prime Minister Jean Chretien was complacent in managing the federal campaign. Mulroney's calls became more frequent and urgent by the day, and I pressed my newsroom colleagues to track developments in Quebec with eyes wide open.

Early October, I visited our bureaus in the west and arrived at my hotel room in Vancouver to a ringing telephone. Mulroney was calling from Montreal to say that, despite the dramatic events unfolding there, he would not be able to call me again for some time. He said no more except to insist that the coming referendum would be close indeed: beware.

That was most strange, given the stakes in play. I assumed he had a serious health issue as he was always saying he expected to die young from a heart ailment, like his father. The hair-raising referendum came and went, with Canada prevailing within one percentage point in the balance, and we spiked the racy editorial written earlier that week in the case of a loss. I heard nothing from Mulroney. I reviewed our standing obituary of him.

Then one Thursday in early November, he called me at home around 11 pm. He said he was on "deep background," meaning I could not directly use any of the information he was about to reveal. Over the next hour, as I took notes, he described a letter that Canada's Justice Department had sent to Swiss authorities earlier that fall, alleging criminal behaviour on his part in accepting cash payments from Karlheinz Schreiber to influence Air Canada's purchase of Airbus planes in 1988.

A copy of the letter had come to him by fax that week, he said, not revealing the source. He went into some detail on its allegations and added it appeared that Maclean's magazine had a copy, based on a list of questions he had received from them that day. Maclean's was set to publish on Monday. "Deep background," he concluded and hung up.

So apparently, Mulroney had wind of this earlier in October (or the fax itself), which is why he called me in

Vancouver, saying he would be silent for a time. Some call; sometimes. He was not dying after all – in so many words.

The next morning, I met with Sylvia Stead, our deputy Managing Editor, and laid out what I knew about the explosive letter and its contents, saying we could use the information only if we could verify it ourselves from other sources. Senior reporters were assigned to the case, whose primary question, sadly, was the identity of my source (which they surely knew). I responded, "Do your job: Get the story!" At the end of the day that Friday, we had no independent information but would surely work hard over the weekend.

I walked over to Yonge Street and St. Clair near my home the next morning and saw a blaring headline in the Toronto Sun about the "Airbus Affair," including all the details from the federal government's letter and allegations against Mulroney to the Swiss. The reporter was Bob Fife, well known to have amazing sources (later Globe bureau chief in Ottawa). Everything I read in the story confirmed what Mulroney had told me on the phone Thursday night. The deep background had become high drama.

This is the one time I called Mulroney of my own volition. With the story fully out in the Sun, I asked him for a copy of the letter so we could match it on Monday morning. He called back to say he would send it to my office Sunday morning on my personal fax number. It then went to our reporters, who were again more fixed on the source of the fax than its contents, but we did publish the basic story on Monday morning in all its gruesome detail. The resuscitated Airbus Affair would be with us for more than five years.

As was a long tradition at The Globe and Mail, I was both editor-in-chief and chair of the editorial board, which produced the daily editorials. I also wrote a Saturday column under my name. On the Airbus Affair, I wrote most of the editorials, based on my knowledge and conviction that a terrible wrong had been done, and also penned signed columns. At the same time, I was ultimately responsible for our news coverage of the affair, with some reporters distinctly skeptical about Mulroney's claims of innocence. Despite my apparent (or real) conflict of interest, I directed the news coverage, which stood objective. That clearly increased tension between me and some in the newsroom, who disliked my double role in news and commentary. Nothing was said overtly, but the tension could be palpable.

Mr. Mulroney sued Ottawa for $50-million in defamation. Allegations of influence-peddling regarding Air Canada's Airbus purchase had been made in the 1980s, and dismissed then after an investigation by the RCMP. Now they returned with a vengeance, backed by the Department of Justice in stark language portraying the former Canadian prime minister as a criminal, and leaked to the world. I asked our news editors to interview everyone at Air Canada in the 1980s who had any role in making the choice of Airbus over Boeing for the planes: board members, executives, senior staff.

Our reporters documented how the choice was made through three evaluation teams at Air Canada, and none of them reported political pressure in making their recommendations: They had chosen Europe's Airbus at a time Canada was negotiating free trade with the United States, and Boeing was lobbying hard through normal channels, as was Airbus. No one on Air Canada's board at that time, including the chair, reported unusual political pressures.

The allegation against Mr. Mulroney was influence-peddling for monetary gain. No influence had been peddled, apparently. There was apparently no crime. Yet the Justice Department claimed a series of payments had been made to him at the time through Swiss bank

313

accounts for acts they had not shown to have existed. I thought this rather shoddy. Nor did they subsequently find a link between Mulroney and the bank accounts listed in the letter.

The case was about to go to Mulroney's libel trial several years later, and I had been subpoenaed by the defence (federal government defending against Mulroney) to testify in Montreal about Mulroney's call to me that Thursday night in 1995. I had no qualms about that. The case fell apart when it was revealed that the lead RCMP investigator had leaked information about the letter to a Maclean's reporter in October, 1995. The defence collapsed, the Crown paid Mr. Mulroney $2-million in costs, and announced that the RCMP would nevertheless continue with its investigation of the former prime minister.

RCMP Commissioner Giuliano Zaccardelli visited The Globe's editorial board sometime thereafter: We had been highly critical of the RCMP's role in the affair together with the Department of Justice. I asked how long the investigation into Mulroney would continue and when the RCMP might inform us of the result. He said the RCMP did not generally state when investigations ended. Incredulous, I noted that this would leave a former

Canadian prime minister twisting in the wind forever, and asked for a promise that the RCMP would publicly inform us of the result of the investigation at its end. We were on the record. He consulted his colleagues and said he would do so in time. I wrote a short editorial the next day recording that promise, which he kept after extensive and expensive months of further sleuthing. The RCMP had found nothing useful to corroborate the Justice Department's letter to the Swiss about Brian Mulroney. Case closed.

I felt pretty good about our coverage of that affair, confirming that years of salacious, airy rumours about Mulroney and Airbus had been put to bed in the absence of any real evidence. Many of my news colleagues did not much like me for it, though I knew. So what? We were in the business of facts, not assumptions.

Imagine my amazement and consternation then when it was revealed in 1999 that Mr. Mulroney had accepted $225,000 in cash from Karlheinz Schreiber after he stepped down as prime minister in June 1993. That he had declared none of it on income taxes. That he said, it was for consulting services after 1993, for which there was no available evidence. And none of this had surfaced after the 1995 letter to the Swiss or his testimony about it at the time? What to make of this?

315

From The Globe's investigations, Air Canada had not been lobbied by Mulroney or his staff or ministers on the Airbus choice in 1988. There was no apparent event. There were no Mulroney-linked bank accounts. Now we had surreptitious cash payments from Schreiber to Mulroney years later as a consultant. The smell test failed.

In several calls, Mulroney offered me several scenarios about the services he had been hired to provide to Schreiber after 1993, including something about a pasta machine. Police and parliamentary investigations revealed no connection between Airbus in 1988 and these later payments and came up cold on why they were otherwise made. Schreiber ultimately went to jail in Germany for illegal political payments there to Helmut Kohl. Mulroney paid his taxes on Schreiber's cash contributions, and that was that, except for the bald facts of the case, which would never go away.

What happened? I do not know. It was probably simple opportunism by both Schreiber and Mulroney – the ultimate networkers - Schreiber buying association with a former prime minister and Mulroney pocketing some easy money when he needed it. Whatever, it cost Mulroney dearly and shadowed those of us too who had defended him so vigorously on the Airbus Affair.

HARVARD CALLING

In October 1999, I got a call from Diane Francis (former editor of the Financial Post) at The Globe, where I was now chair of the editorial board. She had been talking with headhunters for the Harvard Business Review, who were looking for a new editor. She would not be it, but she had recommended they talk to me. I did a video conference with them, then travelled to Boston to meet. We kept talking, and I returned to Boston in early December to see senior business professors and HBR staff at their offices in a suburban business park. On return to Toronto, we agreed that I would return to Boston on January 3 to make the deal. It was an exciting prospect.

Meanwhile, I retrieved numerous back-issues of the HBR from the Globe library to read over the holidays. I went to Conrad Black's traditional Christmas party at his home and pulled University of Toronto President Rob Prichard aside to tell him about these plans and seek his advice. He didn't hesitate to say it was a worthwhile opportunity and stated flatly that I should turn it down. He thought something more challenging for me would surely come around. That was something of a surprise.

At Christmas, I received a call from Brian Mulroney from his home in Florida, who, when I asked, gave the same opinion. He just didn't think the HBR editor would be a good fit, and something else would appear. He wanted me to stay in Canada. That, too, was something of a surprise.

Finally, I consulted my friend Judge Rosie Abella who said immediately: "Take it!"

Over the holidays, I read through many issues of the HBR and decided that seven more years focusing on business and management issues for a monthly magazine, no matter how eminent, was not for me. I called and cancelled my January 3 trip, perceiving some anger on the other end of the line. A few weeks later, talking with my friend Wally about it all, he said, "William, maybe you are just becoming risk-averse as you get older." I replied that turning down the Harvard Business Review at this time in my life, with nothing else on the horizon, was one of the biggest risks I had ever taken. I would be able to assess its wisdom only in retrospect.

The decision was coloured by the fact that I had just taken possession of my newly-built house in the country, on the Niagara Escarpment, 90 minutes northwest of

Toronto in the Mulmur Hills. I was quite prepared to leave that property aside for Boston for some years, but it served as a consolation prize when I determined to stay at home.

***

Before the HBR, risk had never amounted to much in my way of thinking: I simply didn't perceive much risk in making the decisions I did. I grew up at a time of apparently boundless opportunities and options: If one thing didn't work out, something else would come along. And I had never really failed at anything much either, in school or at work. It didn't occur to me that I would be unable to do whatever I set my mind to do, and, in fact, that had been pretty much my story.

I could quit my staff position at Princeton and return to Alberta with no immediate job prospects, not thinking about reputational issues either. Indeed, I could reject several significant job opportunities on my earlier graduation from Princeton to return to Alberta with nothing in view except rejoining my friends making films. I had no lasting doubts as I became editor-in-chief of The Globe and Mail in 1989, without notice or previous thought. Nor did I anguish much jumping across town after 25 years in journalism to assume responsibility in

2000 for Canada's major museum of cultures and natural history, the Royal Ontario Museum.

Young people these days do not live on that kind of cruise control, perhaps. Their world is more competitive, with risks more transparent (though a dynamic digital economy offsets this for some). I rolled along without a plan, tasting options with nary a penny of debt. University graduates today usually carry a mortgage of debt off the bat.

From an unsent letter, March 1, 1970, written from Japan to a friend: "I don't do things. I allow them to happen to me. Things and people happen to me. I have never really done anything. I wait on the sidelines for life to approach me and to humbly offer me its latest offering. All I demand is the illusion of progress."

If I had those laid-back attitudes today, I might well find myself perpetually on the sidelines, waiting for an invitation that would never come. But then, if I were young today, my attitudes would probably reflect the times, and I might be a fierce competitor indeed.

If I did not have plans along the way, I did have ways of doing things – a process rather than a plan: First, do what you really like to do. Second, do it well. Third, things will work out.

PART THREE: MUSEUM

THE ROYAL ONTARIO MUSEUM

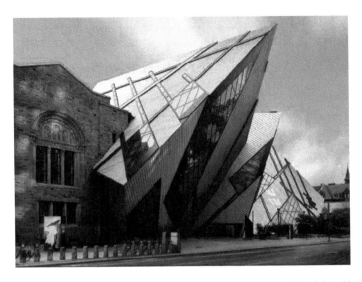

Michael Lee-Chin Crystal, photo credit: Paul Eekhoff, .c.

Royal Ontario Museum

Michael Levine, a prominent entertainment lawyer in Toronto, asked me to lunch in February 2000. He was a Trustee of the Royal Ontario Museum, where they were looking for a new director, and he thought I might be a fit (provoked by a mutual friend, Hugh Brewster, who somehow saw me in that role, and who had led me to buy beautiful land in Mulmur near his property). Levine spoke about enhancing Canadian programming at the museum. I said little; it seemed far-fetched, though I knew Michael to be the man who made things happen behind the scenes.

In March, I got a call at The Globe from Rob Prichard, President of the University of Toronto. He was on the search committee for the ROM director and asked me to meet with the headhunters from New York. I said my interest was tepid – a museum? – but I agreed to meet them for lunch in Toronto later that week. I spent the next afternoon visiting the ROM, where I had not been for some years. Three hours later, I emerged impressed by some collections and perturbed at how much of the museum was neglected and dated, and sometimes simply silly.

I walked around outside the building, which was a jumble of signs, broken pavement and high fences. The next day, I went to the York Club and met the headhunters for lunch.

I told them that I was not a highly motivated candidate for the job, which seemed so far away from my experience. However, I would give them frank views on what I had experienced the day before. I suppose you could say I rather unloaded on them, starting with the display of collections inside, the mood, the maintenance and the sullen face of the museum to the streets.

Having spent quite a bit of time in Paris and London, I gave them a radically different vision of the ROM as I saw it, focused on its major collections in beautiful galleries located in restored heritage buildings, with some kind of dramatic new entry wing facing Bloor Street, where people were actually walking by. I became animated as I found myself envisioning all this, fuelled by anger at the status quo and images of brilliant options, all without much skin in the game.

One of the guys finally asked what similarities I saw between newspapers and the museum, and I blurted out, "The museum is a newspaper in slow motion: It gathers information, brings it to a central location, puts it into some comprehensible order and presents it to the public in a compelling way. The curators and exhibit designers are the newsroom: It is a knowledge factory founded on something more than words, which moves more slowly and lasts much longer." Clear to me.

Finally, in a burst of certitude, I said it would take at least $200-million to tackle the ROM in this way, shook hands, and went back to write an editorial at The Globe and Mail.

An hour later, Rob Prichard was on the phone saying the headhunters were highly motivated, and he wanted me to meet the search committee. I took some background binders on the ROM with me to Paris, where I was travelling with friends. I visited many museums there with a sharpened eye, and met the ROM search committee in Toronto a few days after my return.

Energized by Paris, I gave them the same assessment and vision that I had to the headhunters, insisting that the ROM had world-class collections, which needed world-class treatment in a serious, beautiful setting. The ROM was not a theme museum – it was a collections-based museum that should not lose faith in its core. We lived in a city of people who would throng to such a museum – as they did overseas. If I were to go there, that would be my remit – please write it down – and it would cost at least $200-million. Then I left feeling that a weight had gone from my shoulders.

I went for dinner at the home of my friends Murray Frum and Nancy Lockhart that week. Murray, who was a major player at the Art Gallery of Ontario, took me aside and said he heard that the ROM was talking to me about going there. "Don't do it," he said, "it's a hopeless case and cause – cannot be fixed." I replied that if Toronto elites really felt that way, it was certain to be a self-fulfilling prophecy. On the way home, my motivation to join the ROM surged. Some years later, Murray and Nancy made a significant contribution to the capital campaign.

A week later, the five curators on the ROM search committee of 12 asked to meet for breakfast. They wanted to hear more about my commitment to research and publishing. That was entirely consistent with everything else I had said, and I emphasized again the primacy of collections. That afternoon, Rob Prichard called to offer me the job, subject to reference checks. One of them was Roy Megarry, who had hired me as editor-in-chief of The Globe and Mail 11 years before and was no longer a fan, as I understood it. But he and others apparently came through, and I signed on a few days later.

Phillip Crawley had heard from Roy by the time I told him I was leaving. It was a brief goodbye. The announcement soon after made some waves, surprising as it was to everyone, including me, and provoked many letters of encouragement from a wide variety of people. I would take the first six-week break from work in many years and start at the ROM on August 2, 2000. It would turn out to be among the best decades of my life.

***

At 85 years of age, my father came that same week in June 2000 to see my new house in Mulmur township, northwest of Toronto. He had been a builder himself and, when I sent him the plans a year earlier, he responded by saying the house had too many windows, and would be very expensive to heat: I should collapse the form down to a tight square with small windows. He spoke from experience. I replied that I could afford to heat it, maybe, probably.

Arne went into the house ahead of me to inspect while I unpacked the car of steaks and vodka. "Not bad," he said. A few days later, I found him at the breakfast table with tracing paper, drawing the plan, including the placement of furniture inside so he could show his friends back in White Rock, B.C. The following April, he called to say he had fallen ill. I arrived at the palliative care wing of the White Rock hospital and spent three days reminiscing with him. At one point, he said he wanted a beer. I asked a doctor who replied: "Mr. Thorsell, this is not a prison." I rushed out and bought a six-pack. Arne took a sip and said, "Oh yeah."

We languished through the afternoon until he asked: "Anything more you want to tell me, son?" I answered no: He had long known I was gay, and we had talked about much else in those final days. I asked him the same question. "Well, there is more to tell, but you're not going to hear it," he said with a wry smile. Understood.

We walked the hall as I was leaving and returned to his room, where I hugged him from behind. "Don't say anything," he said, "just go."

Arne passed a few weeks later at 86, healthy just up before the end. He had always said he wanted to die after sinking a birdie on the 18th hole. His wonderful second wife, Rita, was dealing with dementia just then. Her family cared for her well, and she passed sometime later. Full lives lived. Understood.

***

The ROM's Chief Operating Officer, Meg Beckel, had been acting CEO for several months during tumultuous times before my arrival. We went for lunch on my first day, and I said I wanted her to retain many of those same corner-suite duties as COO. My core job as Director and CEO was to realize an extensive rebuilding of the ROM, from old to new, and to help raise the $200-million or so it would take to get it done. I needed Meg to preside over a great deal of the normal business of the museum while I plunged on. She did so brilliantly for the next seven years, and it mattered a lot.

And who knew that one of Canada's best fund-raising professionals had joined the ROM Foundation staff as president just a year before – David Palmer, who also saw us through those decisive seven years until the opening of the Michael Lee Chin Crystal. I arrived at the ROM to find behind the curtain Meg Beckel, David Palmer and several other senior managers of first-rate. Here we go again: more good luck making life better (and some credit to my embattled predecessor as the director, I assumed).

More, the board membership of the ROM Foundation was extraordinarily strong, as was the membership of the ROM Board of Trustees. From the outside, the museum appeared neglected and unloved. Inside, it was rich in human strengths, including most senior management, curatorial staff and volunteers. It did not take long to realize how fortunate I was to inherit the leadership I did behind those daunting walls, and before my daunting ambitions.

I spent the first months at the ROM with three major purposes.

First, the headhunters at Russell Reynolds, and my very wise Trustee Board Chair Stephens Lowden, had briefed me well on the human landscape. When I asked what the first priority was after I arrived, they said "healing." Relationships were apparently frayed at many levels with volunteers, three unions, staff and traditional supporters. I met with Chris Koester, our gentle HR head who had also arrived just a year earlier. We made a pact: All of these relationships would be conspicuously better within two years by documented measures. Chris was a great partner in making that happen.

Second, I wanted to visit every collection held by the museum, whether exhibited in galleries or in the vaults, guided by the curatorial staff in each case. The ROM was a rare universal museum both of cultures and of nature, with significant collections on each side of the mandate. These visits typically took about three hours each and extended well into the autumn. I started with minerals in the deep sub-basement, then on to textiles with 18th Century French court clothing (the people were short). It was intriguing and amazing. Much of what we possessed had no presence in public galleries, including those first two collections. I drove home in the evenings, often appalled at how much of great value was stranded in the vaults, and thrilled at the prospect of bringing the best of it all out into permanent display. This was going to be a revelation. (Later, I devised a weekly ad campaign in The Globe and Mail entitled "What is the New ROM?" that featured one specific collection in a new gallery.) Curators now found themselves at the centre of big plans, some curators skittish after years of being left alone.

At the same time, I explored the museum's buildings and facilities in detail with our building VP, Mike Shoreman and Facilities Manager, Al Shaikoli. I was amazed at the disorder that had been created by renovations decades ago, and by the banality of some of the new buildings. Much needed to be undone before much more could be realized. Looking at the ROM from across the street, I noticed a meagre, tattered, faded Canadian flag flying high over the entrance. I remarked to Al that it would take some years to make the big visible improvements we wanted, but that flag could be replaced tomorrow with something properly sized and ebulliently red and white. It was there the next day as a promise to the future, and we kept it.

Third, I developed a presentation to explain why I was at the museum, and what I thought we needed to do in the years to come. (I was recalling The Globe and Mail: "Why was I hired?") It started with data about our lagging place among major North American museums, financial and attendance numbers, something about our collections, and then a vision for new galleries, the restoration of heritage buildings and a new wing and entrance on Bloor Street. We arranged for every member of the staff of more than 350, from cleaners to professors, to attend these three-hour presentations all mixed up together in groups of about 30. We invited our 500 volunteers and board members to join at will. It took several months to complete the process up to Christmas. I lectured, listened, learned a lot and loved it.

So my first months at the ROM were consumed by me learning about its assets in detail, and ROM staff and volunteers personally hearing my views of the museum and where it needed to go. By January 2001, we had something of a shared understanding of the work ahead, though many people doubted much would come of it, and a few argued that nothing much was necessary in any case. To them, I said, "If we don't change direction, we are likely to end up where we are headed" – not a good place then for the ROM. I was filled with optimism.

***

RENAISSANCE ROM

What we called Renaissance ROM relied initially on our success in applying for Ontario provincial funds under an infrastructure program called Superbuild. Superbuild had set aside $300-million for capital projects in the cultural and recreational sectors across Ontario, to which organizations could apply. The deadline was October 2000, two months after I came on board. Every major cultural institution in Toronto applied, the ROM asking for $50-million as part of its $200-million project. It was part of the deal that Ottawa would match these funds when they were allocated. That would take us halfway.

Stephens Lowden was Chair of the ROM Trustees, who had hired me, and who had shepherded the museum through several years of turmoil in leadership and governance. (Conclusion: accountable management needed to be in charge.) His term was ending, and we needed a new Chair, someone who could help us through this enormous capital project, for which none of us on staff had much experience. Steve suggested Jack Cockwell, former CEO of Brookfield, then a senior strategist there and member of the ROM Foundation Board. It was the Premier's appointment to make, and

Steve assured me that Mike Harris would approve of Jack Cockwell if we could entice him over to the trustees. (Premier Harris had written me a note on my appointment, wishing me well.)

I asked Jack to lunch and made the pitch, saying his experience in finance and development was essential to us, and we had a chance to do something big and influential quite quickly on one of Canada's best pieces of real estate. It was delicate, because The Globe and Mail had focused critically on Jack's company while he was CEO of Brookfield for its convoluted structure and opaqueness. He resisted us quite aggressively at the time – we had a history.

We ignored it now, and Jack agreed to chair the board of trustees for terms that would last six years. I was enormously pleased, as was Premier Harris. We had added the first major new human resource to the Renaissance ROM team, and he was a star. Jack soon became a patient and elegant mentor and, when I went off course, kept my back in a much greater cause. Jack Cockwell is among the lesser-known heroes of Canadian business, philanthropy, education, culture and environment. That story will come out. Jack ultimately donated $10-million to Renaissance ROM.

We set up a task force of Trustees and Foundation Board members to lobby the government on behalf of our $50-million application. Co-chaired by Nicky Eaton and Sal Badali, its members met with every member of the provincial cabinet to make our case. Jack and I started with the premier, and eventually visited all the bank CEOs "just for briefings," as Jack said, though the day would come for asks. We included Liberal and NDP leaders of the opposition, and started over when we had gone through our list once. It was thorough, though we knew the decision would come down to the premier in the end.

In March 2001, our VP Of Facilities, Mike Shoreman, asked when we were going to officially launch the project. I said we had to wait for the results of our Superbuild application, which could take many months. Mike did the enormous service of arguing that we could not afford to wait – that we needed to build momentum relentlessly and publicly, and really start it now. I had earlier announced that we would hold an international architecture competition for the project – the first in more than 50 years for a major building in Toronto. Mike said he could find a couple of hundred thousand dollars in our "rainy-roof fund" to finance it.

On the spot, we decided to proceed immediately and, with board approval and great media fanfare, we announced the competition in June with a deadline for expressions of interest in September. We received 51 letters from architects around the world, and made a long list of 12, from which we would choose three for the last stage. Seven of the 12 agreed to proceed, and we made that announcement to another wash of publicity. (I realized later that we should have started with a shorter list to be fair and effective. At the same time, I eschewed the best-known Toronto architects who were already committed to other major cultural projects, believing we needed to break entirely new ground.)

We would pay $50,000 to each of the three finalists to submit detailed plans, but at this stage, we were offering no money on a proposed budget of $200-million. To be fair, we asked only that firms submit initial ideas on paper, and visit us once in Toronto to explore their ideas. We supplied each applicant with a leather-bound portfolio of vellum paper on which to write or draw what they wished. I wrote a "vision statement" that included restoration of the heritage wings and construction of a new entrance and gallery building on Bloor Street with a condo/museum expansion on the site of the closed planetarium to the south. We added a technical program covering facilities and scope, and hoped for the best.

Within weeks, several firms asked if they could go beyond our paper portfolio and employ other media, including models, at their own expense. Though the deadline for these submissions was late October, we agreed to that, and informed them of all of the changes. We indicated that we would display their proposals in a gallery for public information and comment. Then we waited.

As the deadline came, large crates arrived at our loading dock. Mike, Al, Meg, David and I watched as they were unpacked to reveal these initial proposals, an enormously stimulating process. The first six firms had made models abetted by computer drawings to illustrate their ideas. On the last day, the seventh firm delivered just our leather portfolio back as requested: Studio Libeskind stuck with the original terms of reference and sent 11 drawings on paper – the paper napkins that we used in our restaurant insinuated among the vellum pages. We framed them for display and opened the Renaissance ROM gallery for public view and debate.

There was enormous media interest and public attendance at the gallery. We provided comment cards and tacked them to a large wall at the end of each day, so everyone could share the accumulating debate. We held a packed public forum with media and academic critics.

We established a jury of seven board members and two external individuals – Leslie Rebanks, an architect and brother-in-law to Hilary and Galen Weston, and Belinda Stronach of the famous Stronach clan, who had expressed particular interest (and had the capacity for a significant contribution). Each of the seven firms visited us for identical briefings and tours and to meet the jury. We would announce the short list of three by mid-December.

We made a staff recommendation of three to the jury, of which one firm had to be dropped at the insistence of several members who preferred another candidate. (Independent juries can be terribly independent.) So again, to great fanfare, we announced the short list of Andrea Bruno from Italy, Daniel Libeskind from Germany, and Bing Thom from Vancouver. They would submit models and detailed proposals for another public exhibition at the end of January 2002. Meanwhile, the jury would visit their studios and previously-built works as part of its deliberations. We were moving quickly indeed.

Parallel to this, we conducted a competition to choose a construction manager, who would do the actual building and heritage restoration. We selected Van Bots, and asked them to help evaluate the final three candidates on a technical and cost basis.

We also launched a search for the exhibit designer, who would be responsible (with curators and staff) for the content of the new galleries – some 25 galleries in all. This would be critical in defining the character of the project.

I told each of the three architecture finalists that we would be available for questions as they refined their proposals. Only Studio Libeskind responded: "Can we call you from Berlin next Sunday at 10:30 am your time?" they asked in early January. I made a pot of coffee, and the phone rang: "We have 14 questions for you this week, and wonder if we could call again next Sunday too." The first question was: "When all those school children come into the ROM each morning for their organized visits, what are the first things they do?"

Most of their questions had to do with visitor behaviours and the logistics of exhibitions and programs in a museum with two major mandates. We didn't talk directly about architecture except for one last call from Daniel: "William, do you prefer escalators or elevators?" For cultural institutions, I replied, elevators: Escalators are for shopping malls and airports. We got elevators plus one of the most aesthetically compelling stairwells in the country.

In January, a group of staff and jury members travelled to Vancouver to visit Bing Thom and see some of his built work. We were impressed by his office and large-scale public buildings, including the Chan Theatre at UBC. We continued to London, where the Victoria and Albert Museum had selected Libeskind to design a new wing that had been approved by their board and local authorities. They spent a Sunday morning taking us through the models and design in detail – an imaginative project that was subsequently cancelled for lack of funds.

We went to Manchester to visit the almost-complete Imperial War Museum North, designed by Libeskind, and a compelling structure indeed. We continued to Berlin and toured Libeskind's Jewish Museum, already an international cause celebre. We visited his offices, where staff unveiled their model for the Bloor Street addition, to our fascination. Andy Bronfman, a ROM Trustee, got down on her knees to get a side look and said, "If we build this, there are going to be car accidents on Bloor Street as drivers gawk away." (Flying into Berlin, Andy clutched my hand and said she had vowed never to visit Germany and was very nervous. She remained nervous until we left three days later.)

Then we went to Turin, Italy, where Andrea Bruno used a car plant to display his ideas with computer graphics, and we saw his charming, small office in an ancient building. Finally, it was Paris to visit Bruno's exquisite renovation of a museum there, while we also toured the classic French museums with their exhibit approaches in mind.

On the flight home to Toronto, I had a pretty clear idea of whom would be preferred.

***

Running on a parallel track was our search for an exhibit designer. Caught up in the competition for architecture, I had left this to another VP, who was running our efforts to develop an international museum consulting business. I had not paid adequate attention to the competition brief here or to the long list of potential firms, though I had a clear idea of what kind of exhibit design I wanted: Object and specimen dense, beautifully displayed.

At the end of January, three finalists came to Toronto and made their presentations. Each of them was from the theatrical school of design, with emphasis on multi-

340

media, sensory environments to tell a story. This was precisely what I didn't want for most of the ROM. In the end, I apologized for letting the process get that far in that way, and said we needed to start over by identifying firms that had produced galleries focused on collections, beautifully displayed. It was a bit of a crisis, but central to the whole purpose and nature of Renaissance ROM.

We soon identified three such firms, one in London, one in Leister, U.K., and one in New York. In April, we visited London and Leister, then Leiden in the Netherlands to see the recent work of the Leister Group, which was excellent. Then to New York, where our candidate firm had clearly only skimmed our brief and had little specific to offer. We chose Haley Sharpe from Leister, and especially its lead designer Alisdair Hinschelwood, who would almost live in Toronto in subsequent years. I spent intense hours with Alisdair about the language of our design and then with him and the curators of relevant galleries, shepherded by Dan Rahimi, our essential, erudite director of exhibits.

We had a working meeting at Hinschelwood's studios in Leister, going over details of layout, colours, materials and fonts. I went around the studio introducing myself to the young staff working on our various galleries: "Hi, I'm William Thorsell from the ROM."

Alisdair later said he was glad I had included my last name: He said his staff thought it must be "Says." Caution noted.

Alisdair joined planning meetings at Libeskind's studio in Berlin, we hired perhaps the best exhibit builder in the world from Frankfurt, and started on our first major collections: Canadian First Peoples (the collection almost entirely confined to the vaults), China, Korea and Japan (Japan also absent from public view). We would launch these new galleries three years later on the main floor of the heritage wings, December 2005. (For Canadian First Peoples, we organized an advisory panel of indigenous leaders from major groups.)

I was in a taxi in Berlin thinking of the soaring vault at the centre of the Crystal and pondering suggestions for its use. I realized it connected all four floors and the two ROM mandates of culture and nature in one mysterious volume. I would call it The Spirit House, and animate it with sound and temporary installations. On my departure from the ROM, they named it the "Thorsell Spirit House."

***

COLLECTIONS COUP

Barely three months into my tenure, I got a call from ROM Trustee Joey Tanenbaum, who said he wanted to come for lunch and bring his lawyer. (At The Globe and Mail, this usually presaged a defamation notice.) Joey arrived the next day with Ron Appleby, and insisted we start with martinis, which became a motif for us over the next 15 years. Then a second. Then Joey got down to business.

He and his wife Toby had accumulated the most extensive collection of Chinese art and artifacts in North America, along with important smaller materials from the Middle East. A year earlier, they announced they were gifting the collection to the National Gallery of Canada in Ottawa, despite its lack of depth or expertise in China. Joey said he had taken an intense dislike to my predecessor as Director at the ROM, and simply would not consider the ROM, despite the obvious logic of doing so. Now I had arrived, and Joey apparently approved of what he saw. He said he wanted to withdraw the collection from the National Gallery, who were moving slowly on its reception given their lack of expertise, and give it to the ROM. He estimated its value at around $100-million.

I checked with our curators, who knew the collection very well indeed, and who had been lusting after it for years. We had an enormous coup on our hands – the biggest and finest single addition to the ROM's collections in its history.

There was an important piece of context, however, which explained in part the shift from the National Gallery to the ROM: Joey wanted the collection to be classed as nationally significant by the Cultural Properties Review Board in Ottawa, and registered as a philanthropic contribution under the Income Tax Act before the end of the calendar year – just two and a half months away. Was this possible?

Meg Beckel met in Ottawa with Alex Himelfarb, the deputy minister of Culture and Heritage, who called in his equal in finance. Short story: They and we met the deadlines, and the Tanenbaum collection was ours. It made a big news splash indeed and gave immediate credibility to the new regime at the ROM, and Renaissance ROM itself. (I called Alex Himelfarb to thank him for his decisive help. "You are not calling for anything else?" he asked. I said no, just to thank him. He replied that no one had called him just to say thanks for something in his entire public career. We had dinner in

Rome several years later when he was Canadian ambassador to Italy.)

Big wooden crates began arriving a few weeks later, and I went up to the Chinese vaults to watch the unpacking. There would be a large ceramic horse in one, a fiercely painted warrior in another, ancient pottery bowls (almost art deco) in a third – more than 1,000 works of art. It was a happy coincidence that we were creating an entirely new Chinese gallery through Renaissance ROM, so this amazing gift could be fully integrated into our already famous collection. But that was four years away – too long to wait.

I loved the juxtaposition of the plywood cases, packing materials and priceless artworks within and decided to create a special exhibition titled: "Just Uncrated: Treasures from the Tanenbaum Collection of Chinese and Middle Eastern Art" displayed in and on the crates in which it came. The exhibition opened six months later, plywood crates and all, index numbers hanging on strings from figurines, with simply-typed descriptions on ordinary paper. Joey and Toby Tanenbaum stood beside Premier Mike Harris at the gala opening as the Premier described the ROM as "the people's museum." Indeed it was, now significantly enhanced.

345

Other than securing Joey's tax receipt on time, we faced several other tasks in accepting the collection. We checked every one of more than a thousand pieces for authenticity, and just a handful were found to be forgeries, and were replaced.

Provenance was the other major issue: Where did these artifacts come from, and when? Were they legally acquired and imported? The paperwork indicated that all of them had been legally exported from Hong Kong to the United States before international conventions made trafficking in such goods much more difficult. However, that left many questions about their origins in China. Thus, we did something very unusual for the time: We compiled a list of all the objects with photos, and our curators went to Beijing to seek information from the antiquities authorities there about the collection. Did they have any records of looting or robbery that applied to these pieces? Eventually, the Chinese came back saying they had no such records and, finally, without saying they "approved" of our taking the collection in, they wished us well and expressed their appreciation for our outreach, which they said was unique.

Three years later, top officials from the Chinese National Museum in Beijing visited us in Toronto, and I accepted an invitation to visit them in return as they

346

renovated and expanded their building on Tiananmen Square in time for the 2008 Olympics. They were proud of the quality of the Chinese collection at the ROM and saw it as a valuable expression of Chinese culture in North America. (The Greeks, on the other hand, insisted that every artifact in our Greek collection be examined for possible repatriation claims before they would support any remake of our Greek gallery. I had a beautiful plan for that – and it didn't happen.) I then went to Xian to see the famous Terracotta Warriors. They said I was the first foreigner invited to walk among the warriors in the pit since Bill Clinton, and we mounted our own exhibition from there four years later. (I also spent a week in Japan seeking financial support for that gallery, which included a visit to the site of Expo 70 in Osaka, where I had worked for Canada.)

Finally, we arranged the valuation of the Tanenbaum collection for tax purposes through independent assessors. There was predictable to-and-fro before we came to an agreement with the donor, appraisers and federal authorities. It was the largest single gift by monetary value in the history of the ROM, and the most valuable by far in the quality and quantity of the artifacts. Joey and Toby Tanenbaum subsequently donated $5-million to the new Chinese gallery, which bears their name (as does the Byzantium gallery, another focus of their gifts). Look for their names, ubiquitous, on the labels for artifacts in that gallery: I love the expressive bowls made three thousand years ago and now displayed in Toronto.

I came to embrace the Tanenbaums personally, as Joey and I would have a martini lunch every few months and talk about life, love, history, family, jealousy and art, promising not to tell Toby about the martinis: She had no illusions about those. We made some special bonds, enduring.

***

DANIEL LIBESKIND PREVAILS

Photo credit: Paul Eekhoff, .c. Royal Ontario Museum

Detailed architectural models and drawings from the three finalists arrived in late January 2002, and we showed them in another special exhibit, again with public comment cards. Then each finalist came to present their proposal – first to a public meeting in the ROM, second to the ROM selection committee, and third to our construction managers, Vanbots, who would do a technical and financial evaluation.

The first presentation was from Bing Thom, Vancouver, on a Monday evening in mid-February (during the Olympics). We were gratified with 600 people in the room.

The second was Tuesday from Andrea Bruno, Italy, and, again, we were pleased with 600 people.

The third on Wednesday evening was from Daniel Libeskind, and we had 1,600 people, including many of the city's prominent leaders. We set up TV screens in adjoining spaces to accommodate the crowds. At the front door, a security guard told me we had reached the fire limit in accepting more people, who were still lined up in the snow outside. I went to the volunteer who was clicking in each person, returned to the security guard and said the clicker had earlier broken, and we were fine. Everybody in.

I walked Daniel and Nina Libeskind up the aisle to the stage to robust applause. If this was indeed the people's museum, the people were speaking.

Libeskind made his presentation to our jury the next morning, the last to do so. Then we paused for two weeks while Vanbots produced their comparative analyses of costs and technical issues. Vanbots was, I thought, even-handed to a fault, perhaps careful not to be blamed by the losers. The jury was to meet at 8 am on a Tuesday morning to make its decision, followed by a Trustee board meeting at 11 and a public announcement at 1 pm We had left no room for error or the unexpected.

(The day before, I got a call from Ontario's then-Minister of Culture, Tim Hudak. Our $50-million Superbuild application was still pending, 18 months after its submission, and Hudak had been rather unfriendly to us on that matter. He complimented us on the attention we were getting on the architecture competition, cleared his throat and asked whether, the next day, he might be the one to announce the winner. I agreed on the spot.)

The jury now consisted of only eight members, Belinda Stronach having made none of the meetings or presentations along the way and so disqualified. I felt confident I had the votes for Libeskind, whose presentations met the program, the vision and the technical issues most completely (his was the only proposal that avoided demolition of heritage building assets) – not to mention he was the favourite within the museum and the public. The discussion turned out to be more intense than I expected; one member was completely opposed to Libeskind, one more gently opposed and one suddenly uncertain in the face of the debate. But we ended up with five votes for Libeskind, two against and one abstention – enough to carry the day then made unanimous. It was 10 am

I told my guys to spirit the Libeskind architectural model up to the Glass Room, where the news conference would happen at 1 pm Then, by pre-arrangement, I called each of the finalists with the news. Andrea Bruno essentially hung up on me from Turin. I invited Bing Thom to dinner when next in Toronto to discuss the strengths and limits of his proposal if he wished. He didn't. Finally, I called Nina Libeskind, who answered from an auditorium in London, where Daniel was speaking on stage that very moment. She called her colleagues in Berlin, where champagne flowed.

I arrived after our Board meeting with Tim Hudak at the Glass Room to find maybe 15 TV cameras and a packed house sitting before the cloaked model of the winner. I made a few comments, then handed an envelope to the Minister, who didn't know who the winner was. He fumbled Libeskind's name a bit, but there was a burst of applause as we pulled the cloth off the model. Journalists ran forth to ask the minister if this meant the ROM would be getting its money from the Ontario Government. He demurred, smiling warmly. (One journalist asked me what "Plan B" was if "Plan A" didn't come to pass. I replied that Plan B was to realize Plan A.)

We were top-line national news that evening and next morning, Libeskind the popular choice, but deeply opposed by some. I had argued all along that Toronto in 2002 needed a truly bold statement on the corner of Queen's Park and Bloor Street, after decades of dross and economic recession in the city. The ROM could create a new sense of the possibility in the urban landscape through its choice of architecture alone. I intoned that "Beauty has many faces," and we as a cultural institution had a responsibility to break new ground even as the art of architecture was bursting the bonds of Modernism and the International Style around the world. Toronto already had some of the most beautiful "boxes" in that style at the TD Centre and CIBC bank headquarters downtown. We didn't need another copy-box on Bloor.

I also argued before our boards that if we were to raise $200-million, we needed to create "a landscape of desire" that went far beyond the ROM itself into the heart of city-building. The project could not be just about the museum, rather needed to mark a dramatic change in the ambition of the city as a whole, including a major new public plaza on Bloor Street. We had just run the first international competition for architecture in Toronto in more than 50 years, and produced a radical intervention into the cityscape at one of its most important corners through one of its most important public institutions. True, we had raised hardly a cent for it all as yet, but now we had a vision in the window, which included Canada's biggest heritage restoration project focused on the original buildings and something new and compelling to sell. Our ad campaign said: "Imagination re-creates the city."

I asserted in tandem the importance of presenting all of the ROM's major collections in natural history and arts in beautiful new galleries, liberating many important collections from obscurity in the vaults and vastly increasing the ROM's attraction to the public. We were trustees of world cultures and of natural science and had a serious duty to bring these treasures forward. Our teams were lined up and primed to go: All we needed now was money.

(In this, the ROM was quite different from the Art Gallery of Ontario, which had its major donor, Ken Thomson, already on board, who had a clear desire for Frank Gehry as an architect. At the ROM, we were starting from scratch on the one hand, but had complete freedom of action on the other. We made all our major choices before we raised any money. I wrote a note to Ken Thomson on the announcement of his gift of art and money to the AGO, expressing appreciation for this great act of philanthropy. He called several days later, thanking me for the note, but wanting to make a correction. "You used the word philanthropy, William. I am not a philanthropist. I am moving my gallery from its current location on Yonge Street into the AGO, and paying for that move. That is all." And indeed, those were terms in that case, and Ken was all too influential in guiding the development. Murray Frum, among others, had more visionary ideas for the AGO, but there was no room left around Ken. Murray, like Ken, paid for his own designer to place a gallery within the AGO housing his personal collection of African works. The AGO was populated by donors in a sense the ROM would never be.)

***

David Palmer was President of the ROM Foundation, meaning CEO of its staff, who were responsible for membership, philanthropy and many public programs in support of the museum. He had engaged consultants from Chicago to do a feasibility study on how much we could expect to raise from the private sector for Renaissance ROM. They interviewed 70 people in Toronto over several months and returned to say we should be able to raise between $80-million and $110-million over several years. On that basis, the Foundation board approved the creation of our capital campaign, and David set out to structure and staff it. By March 2002, just after the Libeskind announcement, we had about $12-million in private commitments, most from Foundation board members. David would prove to be among the most potent fundraising executives the country had ever witnessed: He was brilliant at seeing us through other people's eyes, values and aspirations, and very knowledgeable about the core of the ROM. (David went on to be Vice President, Development, at the University of Toronto, where he raised well over $1-billion.)

Toward the end of March, I received a call asking to attend the Premier's office later that morning. I arrived to find my CEO colleagues from the Art Gallery of Ontario, the Canadian Opera Company and the Gardiner Museum of Ceramic Art in the same waiting room. Premier Mike Harris told us we were all recipients of Superbuild support, in the ROM's case, $30-million of our $50-million ask for the first phase of our project. Within minutes, he led us to a waiting news conference and made the announcement public. I rushed back to the ROM to inform our boards and staff.

(Richard Bradshaw was head of the Canadian Opera Company, and we had bonded when I was still at The Globe and Mail. Now we were colleagues and dallied over red-wine lunches at Prego, sharing gossip and strategies on how to raise money, bucking up each other's morale. He would launch Toronto's new opera house with Wagner's Ring Cycle, and I planned a coincident exhibition on Wagner at the ROM, but could not raise funds. Richard died of a heart attack too soon thereafter, leaving no successor of his stature at the COC to date)

The federal government had committed to matching Superbuild Funds and, after much sturm and drang, Prime Minister Jean Chretien made those commitments beside Ontario's new Premier Ernie Eves in late May at Roy Thomson Hall. I returned to the ROM and told our project team we now had $72-million in hand and had no choice but to pull the trigger and start the project in earnest. Then our Trustee Board Chair Emeritus, Liza Samuel, hosted us to martinis on the roof-top bar of the Park Plaza hotel across the street. I looked down to the ROM, knowing that much of what we could see from there was about to change, and more.

357

***

Liza Samuel on Dance Smartly, 2008

David Palmer was focused on ensuring I met everyone who might matter to Renaissance ROM. Liza Samuel had been Board of Trustee Chair in the mid-1990s, continuing her family's deep involvement in the ROM stretching back to Sigmund Samuel in the 1930s. Liza resigned from the trustees when her respected husband, Ernie, fell ill, and he died in the spring of 2000, just at the time of my appointment. Some months later, David suggested we have lunch with Liza, who was emerging again into the world. I called her from my country house to make the invitation. We got along famously.

And so began an excellent friendship with Liza Samuel that went far beyond ROM business, and included wonderful trips on her superb sailing boat, Dance Smartly, in the Caribbean and off the coast of Maine or Cape Cod. Our first trip with Ken and Jean Harrington was off Maine in September 2001, where, on a lovely Tuesday morning, we learned that a plane had hit the World Trade Centre. We were sailing in the islands and did not get a newspaper until the following evening. On Sunday, Liza's company jet was the first allowed to cross into US airspace to pick us up in Bar Harbour for our return to Toronto. It was the first of many adventures with Liza " —adventure" being her favourite word and aspiration.

Liza became close to many of my friends, who came along on these trips. She joined the board of the ROM Foundation, served on the architecture jury and became a major donor to the campaign. Her health was fragile after a life of smoking, and she died in March 2008, still fiercely engaged with the world and furious at having to leave it. Jack Cockwell donated funds to build a green roof at the south end of our new rooftop restaurant, C5, if we named it "Liza's Garden." I became friends with her children and was a trustee of her estate. Liza Samuel's love and friendship were among the most valuable gifts I received from the ROM, and remain with me.

***

With Conrad, Barbara and Rob Prichard at Fort Belvedere

After Jack Cockwell became Chair of the Trustees, we were immensely fortunate to entice Jim Temerty to chair the ROM Foundation (where he was on the board, and where Frank Potter was stepping down). Jim soon converted the Foundation to the ROM governors in closer partnership with the Trustees. (Jim said he had agreed to be chair only after many conversations with his wife Louise, who was integral to all he did.) Jim came to know ROM staff and collections very well and chaired his board with consummate grace, recognizing individuals '

360

activities from memory. No one left a meeting chaired by Jim Temerty feeling anything but a commitment to the cause. Jim and Louise donated $10-million to Renaissance ROM.

We were also blessed when the Honourable Hilary Weston agreed to serve as Chair of the Renaissance ROM Campaign. (She had served as lieutenant governor of Ontario.)

I spent many months seeking Hilary's participation at the ROM, where her family had a long history. At one point, I stood in her office on St. Clair Avenue, overlooking the city on a grey November day and said, "It's depressing. Not much has happened in the cityscape for 40 years. We can make something wonderful happen at Bloor and Queen's Park at the ROM within the next ten years." We had already chosen Libeskind, and she consulted with friends in New York City and London about him. I visited her and Galen at their estate in Windsor, Florida, where I shared Libeskind's plans with them and Queen Noor of Jordan (an American who had studied architecture at Princeton when I was also a student there).

Hilary sent staff to meet with David Palmer at the ROM Foundation to assess our fundraising expertise.

(She was thorough.) David impressed. I spoke with Hilary in London, and she agreed to serve on the condition of meeting alone, separately, with Jack Cockwell and Jim Temerty at their offices in Toronto. I told them I had done what I could, and now it was up to them. She spent more than an hour with each of them, and I never learned what was said, but I did hear the conclusion: Hilary Weston would chair the Renaissance ROM Campaign.

When we made that announcement, the world knew the campaign would be a success, and Renaissance ROM would bloom.

The RenROM campaign grew to hundreds of volunteers organized in committees representing diverse communities in Ontario. Hilary and I met with each of the five major bank chairmen to make our pitch for more money than they wanted to give and ended up with more than $5-million. We flew to Montreal and overcame John Rae's objections to win $2-million from the Desmarais family through Power Corp. We jumped on a little propeller plane to fly from downtown Toronto to Guelph for dinner with the Hasenfratz family of Linamar Corp. (Linda was on the governors 'board.) Hilary saved herself for major calls, approached them strategically and conducted them brilliantly. We had fun.

362

The three chairs alone at RenROM – Weston, Cockwell and Temerty – and their families contributed $40-million to the campaign, which ultimately raised more than $300-million.

(At one point, Galen and Hilary invited me for a weekend at their island "cottage" in Georgian Bay. We flew up on a floatplane during a major storm and landed in rough waters in the bay, where their people boated us over to the house – a superb glass box whose walls were set into the granite of the island, warm wool rugs here and there to cover the rock floor. Here, Galen took me aside and asked how fundraising was going and what needed to be done to assure its success. The Weston family had committed $20-million at that point. I indicated we needed more. Through their networks, they quickly found another $9-million.

I also attended Hilary's birthday party at Fort Belvedere, where they lived on the grounds of Windsor Castle, and which was attended by the Queen. After fireworks set to music, I mentioned over martinis to the Queen that the neighbours might be moved to complain about the noise. "Well, the neighbours are here, actually," she responded.)

**

MICHAEL LEE-CHIN

In the fall of 2002, David Palmer and Jim Temerty visited Michael Lee-Chin, a member of the ROM Foundation Board, to assess where he might stand on contributing to Renaissance ROM (as they were doing with all board members). The Libeskind Crystal was now in the window. We were looking for a naming sponsor for everything, of course, the Crystal being Number One at $30-million. The conversation got around to the Crystal, and they asked Michael if that might be of interest to him. He said something like, "It might not be not of interest."

Well, that was a provocation. David and Jim met with Hilary Weston, and Jim and Hilary arranged to travel to Burlington, Ontario, the head office of Michael's mutual fund company (AIC), to "make the ask," as they say. (At a meeting of American museum trustees in Washington, D.C., a grandee told me the ROM would not raise much money: "Canadians are too nice to make the ask, and if they do make it and get a 'no', they take no for an answer.")

Jim and Hilary arrived the day after Forbes Magazine published its annual list of billionaires. As Michael described it to us all later, Jim and Hilary walked into his office (the Westons were among his business heroes, and he held some of their stock, but had not met them), there were pleasantries, and then Michael showed them Forbes. There, in the middle, was a double-spread layout showing the Westons on one page and Lee-Chin on the other – the Canadian billionaires. "My goose was cooked," said Michael, knowing Hilary Weston was visiting him in Burlington the next day. He said he was amazed that she had come to his office. How could he say "No" to Hilary Weston for $30-million to name the Michael Lee-Chin Crystal after that?

He said he would call Hilary a few days later to respond. David Palmer and I were in her office on St. Clair Avenue that afternoon waiting for the call. The phone rang. Her face beamed. She served champagne.

Michael Lee-Chin had come to Canada from Jamaica at the age of 19 to study at McMaster University in Hamilton. By the time I met him at the ROM, he was the founder and owner of a mutual fund company commanding billions in assets (AIC). He started out by selling mutual funds to Mennonites on farms. He came to my office early on to explain his approach to investing (a la Warren Buffet) " –Buy, Hold and Prosper." And now he was investing in the ROM. He strongly shared my view that Toronto needed a Spark! He was smart, ebullient and optimistic – compelling even. He had a charisma that could be honed but not learned. I was unaccountably proud of him.

We would announce our $30-million naming donor for the Crystal one morning in April 2003 to great media attention. Most everyone expected it to be the Westons (who would be there). We set up a stage with a big screen. This was going to be a coup.

That morning, I got a call at home from David Palmer saying Michael Lee-Chin would not be showing up for the event. Had he backed out of the donation? No. He had brought his mother from Jamaica to Burlington for the announcement, and she had forbidden him to attend. Why? SARs. Toronto was under World Health Organization warnings about SARs, the deadly covid virus that had arrived in Toronto some weeks earlier through visitors from China. Michael's mother feared they would be exposed to SARs if they came to the ROM that morning, so they would not go.

Galen Weston called Michael at home to remonstrate, to no effect. So, under Michael's picture on a screen, we made the historic announcement to a packed house that an immigrant from Jamaica named Michael Lee-Chin was donating $30-million to the ROM to name the Crystal on Bloor – but he needed to be in Burlington that morning

366

for personal reasons. The media could go there to interview him, but he would not be in Toronto.

Few people knew his name, and the QEW to Burlington was soon filled with journalists to find out who he was.

It was marvellous that our first major contributor to Renaissance ROM was a little-known immigrant to Canada from Jamaica. It created a new sense of the possible and unsettled the consensus in cultural Toronto to my delight: The Michael Lee-Chin Crystal. (Over at the somewhat intimidated AGO, they stopped ribbing it as "Billy's Crystal.") A radical architectural statement in Toronto by a man who had designed the Jewish Museum in Berlin had been embraced by a black immigrant to Canada who loved the structure's vision, and who had been inspired by the former lieutenant governor of Ontario. Michael made good on that pledge, and the Michael Lee-Chin Crystal stands as a defining moment in Toronto's evolution: not another box in the big sense of the word.

Some months later, we made the announcement of the Weston contribution to the ROM. I went to their townhouse on Eaton Square in London to learn they would contribute $20-million – half from Hilary and Galen personally, and half from the Weston Family

Foundation. The 1932 building on Queen's Park would be named after the Westons. It was important they not be seen to challenge or overshadow Lee Chin's gift. Of course, Hilary, as chair of the campaign raised a great deal more.

Great cities result from the encounter of many happy circumstances, including smart public authorities allocating public funds. (Mike Harris told me his proudest legacy was the creation of Waterfront Toronto Corp. and the capital funding of Toronto's major cultural institutions.) When I arrived at the ROM in 2000, Toronto also possessed substantial private wealth and an impulse toward major philanthropy. Within one decade, its cultural institutions, including the Royal Ontario Museum, Royal Conservatory of Music, Gardiner Museum, National Ballet School, Canadian Opera Company and Art Gallery of Ontario raised more than $1-billion from the private sector alone to remake those institutions – far more than from the public purse. Since then, universities, hospitals and other good places have raised billions more. Philanthropy supports decisive initiative at the edges of knowledge, compassion and creativity, a foundation of our culture.

***

MUSEUM BUILDING

Toronto did not need more boxes, Photo credit, William
Thorsell

Working with Daniel and Nina Libeskind was
enormously stimulating and sometimes frustratingly
non-linear. Daniel's mind darted around, and it was not

always easy to go quietly over practical options and developments. Besides, they soon won a competition to be master planners for Ground Zero in New York, the World Trade Centre site, and their attention was drawn away.

I too quickly accepted a proposal to alter the exterior cladding language of the Crystal in response to issues of snow and ice on slanted surfaces. This offended the public sense of what the Crystal meant and caused chronic debate. Later in the project, I failed to win public support for a combined ROM extension and condominium on the site of the closed planetarium, which was part of the original vision and financial plan. (We eventually sold the planetarium to the University of Toronto, with the right to lease ROM space in any new building there.) That did not go down well with some members of my boards, whom I did not always adequately consult. There were times on operational matters when I should have been better connected, focused and impactful on the ground.

At the first formal meeting of the architects, construction managers and ROM management, the chair suggested that everyone probably had one major question they wanted to ask. "Let's start with Mr. Thorsell," he said. I had to come up with a question fast, and it was this: "You architects and construction people are here because you are obviously very successful in your fields. We at the ROM have not done this before. What's makes for a good client?" So, "Over to you, Mr. Libeskind," replied the chair. "A good client knows what he wants, why he wants it, and speaks with one voice," said Daniel. That is not the only test, but we did pass it.

Libeskind made a memorable intervention at the outset when we were meeting with engineers and builders about the steel structure and cladding of the Crystal. The lead engineer from Arup in London spoke for an hour about unprecedented problems in realizing the design. (The cantilever over Bloor weighs many tons. There could be avalanches.) Suddenly, Libeskind banged his hand on the table and said: "Problems, problems, problems! You have spent an hour describing nothing but problems! We have no problems!" There was a pause, and the imposing engineer said, "Well, Mr. Libeskind, what then do we have?" Daniel replied, "We have puzzles! People run away from problems but go out and buy puzzles. We have puzzles – puzzles are intriguing and can have beautiful solutions!"

I called a pee-break, and the "P" word at Renaissance ROM became Puzzle, whatever the challenge at hand. It was perhaps a bit fey, but it did alter the atmosphere when crises hit, which they surely did. Try it at home.

At a public forum on the design, a woman stood and said: "Mr. Libeskind! We have been building beautiful buildings in our culture for thousands of years using right angles: 90 degrees! Every wall in your crystal here is slanted – even the floor is slanted. What's wrong with 90 degrees?" Daniel strode to the mic and said: "There is nothing wrong with 90 degrees, Madam. There are, however, 359 other degrees, surely worth exploration. We are doing that here." He got applause for that, but many people still don't agree.

During construction, we encountered the usual litany of "puzzles," including exploding steel prices and shortages of many components imported from abroad. Expensive change orders plagued renovations and new designs. Our rate of fund-raising did not always coincide with that of our billings, so an occasional Friday evening was taken up with the bank to pay project costs (what's a million?). Meanwhile, I personally guided hard-hat tours through the site for every member of the ROM staff, volunteers and boards, twenty at a time, each one receiving a Renaissance ROM T-shirt and RenROM hammer at the conclusion. There would be no retreat on this.

Our curators and exhibit designers worked under Dan Rahimi and Alisdair Hinschlewood to present the collections in some of the most beautiful settings in the world. Their intellectual rigour was central to our particular aesthetic design. There is no hiding the result.

We opened the first phase of Renaissance ROM in December 2005 in the renovated main floor heritage buildings – including restoration of the 1932 rotunda on Queen's Park, the Currelly main hall and new galleries of Canadian First Peoples, China, Japan and Korea. (We removed the walls and windows in the 1914 wing along Philosophers Walk and restored its link to Currelly.) Princess Takamado came from Japan for the opening gala of the gallery named after her late husband, who had studied at Queen's and died of a heart attack playing squash in the Canadian embassy in Tokyo. We opened the Michael Lee-Chin Crystal on Bloor Street in June 2007, with an outdoor concert extravaganza produced by David Foster before tens of thousands of people, including the governor-general of Canada and Premier of Ontario.

The Globe and Mail's architecture critic shredded it, and hoped it would be demolished within 20 years. At the same time, it was celebrated in many publications internationally. It polarized people, many of whom in Toronto I knew, and some of whom shunned me for it. More than a decade later, it is a beacon of art in the cityscape to many and a continuing affront to others. Still now, I thrill at it, inside and out, confident at its place in history and the city, as you might expect.

(A few months later, I received the Order of Ontario, which I accepted explicitly on behalf of the ROM community.)

***

Four days later, I chaired a dinner meeting of the Grano Salon, a club of Toronto's establishment figures, sponsored by Peter and Melanie Munk, that met at Grano restaurant to hear talks by famous people on public policy. Our guest in June 2007 was Gore Vidal, and the topic was "Whither Europe?" The night before, I went to dinner near the ROM with Vidal and Rudyard Griffiths and Patrick Luciano, who ran the Grano Salon, and who had asked me to moderate the evening.

Vidal arrived in his wheelchair with a handsome young aide and ordered the first of many scotches. He dominated the conversation entirely with a series of well-rehearsed perorations on the decadence of the United States and various individuals he had known. As we left the restaurant around 11 pm, I said to my hosts that the next night's conversation with Gore Vidal on Whither Europe would be neither a conversation nor anything much to do with Europe.

Indeed, after I introduced Vidal with a question about Europe, taken from one of his recent books, he launched immediately into a rant about Conrad Black, whom he knew was a member of the club then residing in an American prison. I posed a second question, and he reverted to the first of his raves about American decadence. At this, I turned to the audience and said, "Let's just leave him to it, shall we?" to applause, and he did an encore of the previous night. Gore Vidal's famous personage had its privileges, and he always used them. I didn't like him much.

We had more galleries to build and thus to fund. David Palmer connected with two more donors who made major contributions.

The first was Donald Lindsay, CEO of Teck Corporation, the big Canadian mining company based in Vancouver. We proposed they fund a new gallery of minerals, gems and jewels, along with the Canadian Mining Hall of Fame. This would liberate the ROM's stunning mineral collections in a gallery of some 10,000 square feet as Chapter One in our second-floor story of life on Earth. David drew up a $10-million proposal for consideration of Teck's board meeting in Vancouver. We sent it on and stood by to fly out on short notice to make the case. Instead, we got a call saying the Teck board had agreed to it all the next morning. At the public announcement, Don Lindsay revealed that he had attended Saturday Morning Club at the ROM as a boy, and that his mother had been a long-time volunteer. He knew value wherever it showed its face, and the Teck Gallery is among the most beautiful for minerals in the world.

At the same time, David built a connection to Robert Shad, an immigrant from Austria who had built an enormously successful engineering firm in Ontario serving the automotive industry. He was also a fervent environmentalist, the creator of Earth Rangers, an influential centre for public education just north of Toronto. David and I visited him there, amazed by his passion for nature and concern for its future.

We proposed that Robert fund a $10-million gallery of biodiversity – the last chapter of our narrative starting with minerals, leading through early life, dinosaurs and early mammals on the second floor. He responded, insisting there be a strong emphasis on "life in crisis," which we embraced. David presented our proposal to Robert at the Earth Rangers centre and called to say Robert was not happy with $10-million. "Good try," I said: No! Robert insisted we accept $2-million more to endow vigorous programming in the studio we planned within the gallery. It had to be $12-million or nothing! (Robert said later he had never thought of funding any museum until he saw the steelwork going up on Bloor Street for the Michael Lee-Chin Crystal. If they are thinking like that, they might be worth a look, he concluded.)

We established a team to plan the gallery, which opened some two years later (after a surprise visit from Prince Andrew, who dropped by the ROM one morning with an attractive young woman and visited the unfinished installation.) Robert was not impressed. The "life in crisis" message was far too subtle in his view, and I had to agree. This led to efforts to amplify that message, including the appointment of a senior manager to program the studio within. We negotiated these corrections over excellent wine at the home of Robert and Liz Shad, who remain transformative forces across many dimensions in Ontario.

Ultimately, we raised more than $200-million from private sources, none of whom reneged on their pledges of support in the end. In all, including public support and gifts in kind, we raised some $330-million for Renaissance ROM, a third of a billion dollars.

By 2010, we had completed 27 galleries, while producing a vibrant, uninterrupted series of special exhibitions and programs, never closing the ROM down. We created a program to showcase Ontario regional museums at the ROM. (My favourite major exhibitions: Scythia, Art Deco, Canada Collects, Darwin, Vatican Museums, Dead Sea Scrolls and Terracotta Warriors. I also loved our boutique exhibit on typewriters.) Jim Temerty inspired another ROM exhibition on the Trypillian people of pre-Ukraine, and we visited the President of Ukraine in Kyiv to source the artifacts. We returned to Toronto one day early, encountering a ROM patron in our hotel lobby who gave us a lift directly over the Arctic on his Challenger jet.

In 2008, Ontario doubled its annual operating support of the ROM, and our attendance was breaking through one million on the way to a promised 1.4-million after completion.

In 2006, I attended a week-long congress marking the 500th anniversary of the Vatican Museums in Rome. I was on the final panel with the directors of the British Museum and Louvre. I titled my presentation: "The Museum as the New Agora," arguing that great museums now provide critical common ground in multicultural and increasingly secular societies – a kind of town square that resonates more broadly than almost everywhere else. (An older man jumped to his feet after my presentation and shouted: "Now I understand!") In our audience with Pope Benedict, I said I was from Toronto. "I have great memories of Toronto," he said, having visited several times as Cardinal Ratzinger. I liked the Vatican and thought that, had I been Catholic, I might have fallen for that fey, privileged theatre of life.

Several months later, I gave the same speech to the Canadian Club in Toronto. Melanie Munk was in the audience, and within two weeks, she and Peter donated $2-million to Renaissance ROM. That was evidence of the agora indeed.

I made a particular commitment to the Institute for Contemporary Culture at the ROM, an excellent inheritance from the 1990s. I insisted that museums exist in the present and future, as well as past, and dedicated a wonderful top-floor space in the Lee-Chin Crystal to our mission to keep abreast of the times. That is what a brilliant museum does, and the ICC re-launched with an exquisite exhibition by Hiroshi Sugimoto. The ICC functioned under its own staff and board led by Kelvin Browne and Ron Graham. I particularly liked the exhibition on urban graffiti based on Toronto's homeless tent encampments, and our presentation of El Anatsui, from whom we purchased a major work for the gallery of Africa. The ICC also presented an electric "Evening with Meryl Streep" reviewing her oeuvre in film with Johanna Schneller from The Globe and Mail: Even Ms. Streep appeared entranced.

It seems miraculous in retrospect that we did all this within a decade from a standing start. Every significant collection, except Modern Design and Early Life on Earth, now had its own permanent gallery – all the assets of the museum finally presented to the public in new surroundings. (Early Life has arrived.) Now, the challenge is to power these galleries with story-telling, illuminating them intellectually and emotionally. That surely includes digital tools.

Through these often disruptive times, our Department of Museum Volunteers (some 500 people strong) showed amazing resiliency, as did our teachers who kept the student programs fully functional. Our events staff produced untold galas, private dinners and VIP tours while earning millions by hosting weddings and corporate events off-hours. I embraced the security and front-of-house staff who presented the human face of the ROM to visitors daily. (Who knew how many guards made their own tomato sauce from backyard gardens?)

The heritage renovation restored the virtues of the first buildings fronting Philosophers Walk and Queen's Park. And Libeskind's Crystal created radically new and deeply engaging forms at the centre of Toronto's civic life on Bloor Street – architecture of strong psychological, intellectual and poetic depth. Now almost all the ROM's collections were exposed to public view. By 2010, the ROM was fully functional and contributing to a revival of the whole Bloor Street precinct, an ebullient part of Ontario's public life, I thought. We had realized the vision set in 2000, but I knew there was unfinished business and room for improvement on this marvellous fresh palette. That would come.

PART FOUR: INTERREGNUM

LIFE AFTER SUITS, TIES AND STRUCTURES

Approaching my tenth anniversary as Director and CEO, I thought I might stay on four more years to the ROM's 100th birthday in 2014 when I would be 69. That would be natural, and I felt the draw. But I didn't.

I departed the ROM in doubt about leaving what Hal Jackman once described as "a sacred place," sacred in concentrating evidence of such intelligence in the natural and human worlds in one realm. The ROM was also family to me by then, all who worked there, all who came to visit. To a man living alone, this mattered. And the ROM played an important role in the life of a great city and beyond. I was employed in a marvellous context with much left to do. Staying on was almost in the cards.

All this was true, but some time soon, I would be leaving in any case. The "whether" had to deal with the "when." Life presents this dilemma no more consequentially than older age when time budgets run tighter.

Also, I believed in the principle that, after a decade, both the ROM and I would do well by new circumstances – belief in some kind of cyclical refreshment. ROM boards were changing along with an agenda for the future. New players were emerging with new perspectives I sensed I might not share. I may have been wrong about that, but again, it was only a matter of time. Nevertheless, I have missed the ROM in ways I never missed journalism or The Globe and Mail. I left the ROM wanting more – of them.

At 65, my health was good. I had been working on wonderful assignments for 40 years. I decided to break from formal work to see what it was like to live in a world without external obligations and schedules. This would be the first time I was not "reporting" to someone else – my parents, my teachers, my boss, the public mission. I would be reporting only to myself in a mysterious process yet to be defined. I wanted unfamiliarity and uncertainty again at 65, akin to a younger man's age: more contingency. I wanted some distance from the madding crowd, more time for reflection and impulse both, more privacy perhaps. Who knew how it would go? Goethe again: "The condition of freedom is risk."

***

It is disorienting to plunge from active work in the community to unstructured private time, particularly when you live alone. Predictably, there are issues of self-worth and social regard that can be deflating. But those post-career days will come to almost everyone, which means most of us will have a new job - reporting to ourselves.

I loved graduate school at Alberta and Princeton – the easy camaraderie, the informal schedules, the daily learning and growing of new capacities. I decided this next phase of life would be another graduate school, of which I was both the Dean and only student. I would seek to revive many of those earlier pleasures. I would create an interesting curriculum for myself and get on with it.

Most dramatically, I decided to buy half of a wonderful mountaintop property on the west coast of Costa Rica with Bill and Melody Duron, friends I met in Mulmur. They had been seeking somewhere far south to go in winter. They found a small hotel for sale in Costa Rica, newly built in 70 acres of tropical forest. We rented this remarkable place for a month in January 2010 to explore the possibilities, and bought it in February as a home. I, too, wanted to live outside Canada in winter, in a foreign culture, where I would need a new language and encounter a different social dynamic. (I could not abide the cloying medium-security institution known as Florida or its ilk in the USA.) Costa Rica fit the bill, and these 70 acres of paths overlooking the Pacific were superb.

Several years later, I was best man at the wedding of our property manager there, Marlon Matamoros, to Berna Ugalde, and I am now godfather to their son Albert.

I would also spend time at my country house north of Toronto while in Canada for eight months of the year. I kept a small apartment in the city, not far from Moore Park. These places are well-tailored to my preferences and allow for flexibility as seasons and circumstances change.

I wanted to tackle things where I might improve (not weight-lifting). I started studying Spanish – a fresh pleasure. I devote two to three hours each day to the piano, which I have played all my life, my original 1973 Yamaha grand now in the country. I returned to composing music, and developed a good reading list in the sciences, biography and public policy. I found a one-hour bicycle circuit at my country-house in Ontario, sweeping through farms and dales many days before lunch. I climbed the mountain with our dogs every afternoon in Costa Rica, did some writing, cooking and sipping of Sauvignon Blanc. I joined the board of the Luminato Festival of Arts and Creativity in Toronto and became associated with the Munk School of Global Affairs and Massey College at the university. For three years, I chaired the jury of the Gelber Prize for best book on international affairs in the world. (We awarded first prize to Plutocrats by Chrystia Freeland in 2013, and she enhanced the jury the following year.) I joined the Advisory Board of the Toronto Board of Trade. I did some consulting with a leadership development firm headed by David Anderson. In sum, I constructed my own graduate school and stuck pretty well to a discrete plan of action on the penalty of severe looks in the mirror each morning from the Dean.

I was disappointed not to find more connection with business boards and such, but, as one guy said to me at a party, "William, you are a toxic demographic today – a privileged white man of a certain age." So "OK, Boomer." And there was baggage from various careers, though I might not know its full extent. I could be sharp in conversation, breaking dishes not to be repaired. (Many people are more fragile than I realize, and me more pugilistic.)

And I remained, since 1982, living alone, now without the camaraderie of the workplace and organized life in the community (or even a real graduate school). But managing that fact is part of the assignment. For something of an introvert, it has a certain flavour.

Vivian Gornick once wrote: "When asked about how women might gain greater sovereignty, [George Eliot] urged the women of her generation to employ 'the steady command of thought.' By which she meant: Spend the time alone not in the state of fretful loneliness but in the company of your own working mind, for that is the road to inner freedom. If we are to boil down the benefits of the therapeutic age to a single instruction, that, for me, would be it."

the silly

mystery

of the rose

in the snowbank

is all quite clear

now:

it must have been a

plastic

rose

that some kind old woman

left

in her

loneliness

on her

lover's

grave

November 1972

In writing a memoir, you spend a lot of time in your own working mind and realize that everyone you have been in life remains part of your composite individuality now. Happy memories must never become the source of sad regret, rather accumulate and thrive within each moment. I am grateful that my ebullient 17-year-old self remains just below the surface of the skin. He lives, so the rest of me may.

***

I have enjoyed unusual projects and start-ups, usually in major institutions, close to the centre of things. Being unhappily gay in youth put me once-removed from the world for good and sad. I encountered fields rich with opportunity, just ahead of the baby boomer cohort, riding waves of social progress perfectly suited to my inclinations. I grew up in a functional Scandinavian-Canadian family in quite a homogeneous Alberta, which provided a balance of support, privacy and freedom to let me be and become. I was forgiven much and escaped close calls. In the end, I wonder if life was actually too easy, at the cost of empathy, productive anger, or simple awareness. But at least I wonder.

Emerging from childhood, we grow from me, to us, to them, to humankind. At best, we become "citizens of the world." And then perhaps, we grasp the immensity of nature and the universe and something of our place in it – not just our place, but our sliver in time. That journey can lead to an inner peace, whatever daily circumstance prevails.

My generation, born after 1945, has seen more discovery about the nature of the universe than any except the one that immediately preceded it. We know where we fit in cosmic space and time and how we are made, initially from stardust. We know about the conditions of the universe's birth and how it will end, while still debating its provenance. Our brief window is, in fact, the universe becoming conscious of itself, in us. No generation has come more assuredly into that consciousness than ours. Comprehending the vastness of space-time is not to feel small, rather to thrill at being part of something immense. We are a spark of the ages.

In our careers, we start by being observed, guided and measured. Eventually, if fortunate, we are heard and respected, then respected and empowered, then empowered and indulged, then tolerated, then ignored and finally forgotten. (It is said you only actually die the last time a person says your name: Jesus, Beethoven, Einstein, Hitler and Houdini live.) The latter stages of this arc can be difficult, but they deliver a freedom akin to childhood, a fate to be inconsequential again in wonder at the world. A sense of wonder is the defining attribute of childhood, and its revival a condition of youth.

So we land in this interregnum to ask: What's next?

***

CODA

Cerro Coyote, Costa Rica

The first 21 years of the 20th Century were terrible on balance, defined by the First World War, the Russian Revolution and the flu pandemic that killed millions of people. The next 25 years were worse, including the Great Depression and Second World War leading to the communist takeover of China.

The first 21 years of the 21st Century have been dark as well, starting with 9/11, provoking disastrous wars in the Middle East generating millions of refugees, growing instability in Africa, the retreat of democracy

391

everywhere, including the United States, global warming and the COVID pandemic. The next 25 years of this century do not suggest grounds for hope of improvement.

The Baby Boomers lived their lives largely between these epochs, from 1945 to the early 2000s, in generally robust circumstances. It is worth registering that fact clearly, in gratitude and, perhaps, regret.

CPSIA information can be obtained
at www.ICGtesting.com
Printed in the USA
BVHW091429150322
631522BV00014B/1121

9 781915 206961